DAVID'S HEART

Laurie O'Brien

David's Heart
Copyright © 2022 by Laurie O'Brien

All rights reserved. No part of this publication may be reproduced, distributed, or transmitted in any form or by any means, including photocopying, recording, or other electronic or mechanical methods, without the prior written permission of the author, except in the case of brief quotations embodied in critical reviews and certain other non-commercial uses permitted by copyright law.

Tellwell Talent
www.tellwell.ca

ISBN
978-0-2288-8121-6 (Hardcover)
978-0-2288-8120-9 (Paperback)
978-0-2288-8122-3 (eBook)

Chapter 1

I find myself being more deliberate about everything these days, like taking the time to look at the sky, watch the wind, and hear the animals foraging for a snack. Unfortunately, I have more time on my hands now. My David was my life for a long time but not long enough—thirty-four years, eight months and 26 days. The number 26, like every number, has significance. Angelically speaking, it means it is an opportune time to find one's happiness and peace. I hope so for his sake, as he had a lot of pain and was mistreated by so many. They say that losing a child is the worst thing one can go through, and let me tell you that, unfortunately, it is true. Losing my David, my first-born son, my best friend, my first love in many ways, and sometimes my fiercest opponent was so devastating that I still feel the effects after almost three years. I've heard that one never gets over it; one can only try and get through, knowing there is no end in sight. I hate it, so I look for distractions to shift my mind and thoughts, even for a few moments, as it is a relief. Grief and sadness weigh on me like an anvil, like a dark cloud encompassing me.

David and I when he was around four years old.

When you have children, they become your life and every aspect of your life changes because it's no longer only about you anymore, especially when they are young. When my David was diagnosed with his disorders at 12 years of age, a rollercoaster of life-altering changes occurred for all of us, especially our dear David. Looking back on it now, it was so hard at times that I wondered whether we would get through it, but it was so worth it. Most people do everything to help their children become good human beings and thrive, but what happens when everything isn't enough?

Nowadays, I feel much more aware of everything around me. I'm not overly sensitive; I just seem to notice more. A huge hole left by David's passing is an understatement. He was such a constant in our lives—taking care of him, worrying about him, laughing with him, fighting for him and sometimes with him, but primarily loving and admiring him. Grief takes on different forms, not just stages, like you've heard before. You change the way you do most things in your life; how can you not? You sometimes get impatient; you want people to get to the point and get on with things. You think, "I don't have time for this; I have to get back to grieving." It's where you want to be and where you feel close to your lost loved one. LOST—what a word, you know where your loved one is. I can't even imagine not knowing where one's loved one is from kidnapping or running away. Not knowing if they are alive must be unbearable. How do people survive that?

Some people become disconnected from the rest of the world, which can lead to depression in many cases. At this point, I'm considering counselling, but I have heard from some that it's a waste of time while others say it was helpful. You must be open to it like anything else. I might try it; it's not like my grief is going away anytime soon. I discovered that many communities have special groups for parents who have lost their children, which is good because it's a different kind of pain and loss.

I'm lucky to have supportive people in my life—my husband, David's stepdad Ray, has been my rock, as was our son Kyle. My beloved 94-year-old mother adored David and took care of him when I lived at home with him when he was young. Then there is my wonderful family, friends, and co-workers. My job helped me through this a lot; it was a distraction that I so desperately needed. It helps to focus on other things for periods of time because when you lose someone you love so deeply, they are always at the forefront of your mind.

I find myself wishing for a miracle, wanting David to come home. Do I want him back so he could suffer some more? Can I have him back as a healthy young man? These are the desperate thoughts of a heartbroken mother. I don't pretend to be a grief expert; I'm far from it, but I only know what I'm living. However,

I wonder whether grief and loss differ depending on who you lost or how you lost them. Or is it all relative or the same? I've known people who have lost people to accidents, illness, terrible suicides, and senseless tragedies that can shake you to your core. Thank God I haven't known anyone who has lost someone to violence. I don't even want to imagine what that must be like, but it happens often worldwide. There is also the question of when you lose someone who lived their life and has died at an elderly age versus a young person or someone in between. Does that influence the intensity of our grief? I think it does. Do you mourn someone who was killed in a sudden car accident as you would someone who died of old age after living a full life?

Love and family make our world better. We all know someone who doesn't have anyone, which is sad. Losing a loved one leaves a hole in our lives, but how close we are to that person determines how much our daily life will be affected. With myself and our family, David was with us for almost 35 years—with me mostly and Ray since he was five. When your children grow up, they leave home and start their lives, which is how it is supposed to be, but David was the center of our lives every day of his life. It's hard not to miss the ordinary and mundane things as much as the special times like birthdays, Christmas, trips, and especially concerts! David loved music, all music, even some opera! A lot of people didn't know that. He also loved AC/DC. They were his absolute favourite. He would listen to them daily, sing, and play air guitar. I miss the music, his laughter, and his dry sense of humour.

They say that "grief is love with nowhere to go." That is so true! What do you do when you can't cry anymore? It actually hurts; you get headaches, feel dizzy, and have pain in your stomach. I cried so much the first few months that I dissolved the rubber nosepiece on my glasses. It was the salt from my tears, I guess. The tears came on so suddenly at times that I didn't think to take my glasses off. I couldn't figure it out at first, but I'm sure that's what happened.

Now onto my boy. Where do I start? At the beginning, I guess. David was a bright and curious go-go-go child. I had him at 18 when I was still living at home. We were there for the first three years of his life. My parents were wonderful, although my mom sometimes doted on him too much. I guess it's because she didn't have a boy. I worked full time, and my parents grew very close to him, and he adored them too. With the help of a good friend, I got my first apartment when David was three years old. It was hard being on my own, but I learned. Later, I moved to a townhouse near the church I always went to, and David started kindergarten at the school near the church. He was happy and made a few friends.

David when he was around 8 years old.

Unfortunately, his school years started to be challenging, but I thought it was somewhat normal—boys will be boys. He wouldn't pay attention as well as he should have and started getting into fights, so I was at the school a few times. Later that year, I met Ray, and after a while, we moved in together and away, so David changed schools. At this time, ADD and ADHD were becoming the go-to diagnoses for any kid with any issues. David was labelled troublesome but smart. He would get his work done quickly and would start talking and fidgeting. What I'm saying is that any rambunctious kid was a problem. How did they deal with these types of children back in the day? It makes you wonder.

Months went by, and he was paired with a teacher's assistant for one-on-one instruction, but it also came with problems. David was ostracized on the playground, so keeping friends was a challenge. After some long talks and counselling from teachers and our doctor to take David to a psychologist, I finally consented. However, it wasn't what I expected it to be. Instead of speaking with David, the doctor prescribed different medications for ADD and ADHD. That was the height of these new diagnoses in the late eighties and early nineties. David was put on Ritalin for a while, one of the more popular ones then, and at least five others for about three years. There was only a mild improvement in his behaviour, and he was very withdrawn and quiet at home, so the school sent him to a special day program at a special needs school out of town. They wanted him to do a weekly program, stay overnight, and come home on the weekends, but I said no. It helped somewhat; he was a little more confident, but that could have just been general maturing. I don't know! We put so much stock into what doctors tell us to do because they're the experts, right? Wrong! You are the expert on your child, and the same goes for yourself when it comes to your health. I wish I would have stuck to my instincts back then because God only knows what kind of effect those medications had on my dear boy in the long run.

After about a year, David was back at his regular school with a special education teacher most of the time. He started walking strangely, and I remember taking him to the clinic once to see if he had chicken pox—which was going around at the school—and the doctor asked how much David had to drink! He called it a "drunken gait." I was horrified, but it brought to light that there was something off. At the time, I just thought David was at an awkward stage; in a million years, I never thought it would be the catalyst for something we could never have anticipated, a nightmare in the making. I told my family doctor what the clinic doctor had said and she told me I should report him, and I did.

His walking started getting worse, especially near the end of the day. We thought it was an awkward stage or he was "probably seeking attention—as his pediatrician said—but it wasn't. He was under the top pediatrician's care, but I wasn't satisfied; it was just more pills, and nothing was helping. His behaviour escalated, and he started lashing out at us. He would have outbursts of rage that he could not control. It was very scary and confusing. We think it was all the medications he was on. David was like a guinea pig for the doctors. It's not like today, where you need to ween off certain things. I even called the police a few times. I thought it would scare him, but he didn't care. He would break things and yell and scream for what seemed like hours. Then he would calm down and be still but not remorseful. He was getting his anger out, and that was the result. It was like he was a different person. Thank goodness it didn't happen too often. When he was around 11 or 12, we put him in the psychiatric ward at the hospital for a three-day hold to monitor his moods. This was a pivotal part of his life and ours because I think he thought he was reaching his breaking point. He hated it there, of course, but he didn't fight it. I think he wanted help at that point. I hated having him in there. No parent wants their child in a place like that. On top of the obvious issues of having your life disrupted, it was the belief that somehow you failed as a parent. You feel that way for a bit, it's human nature, but you are not the issue; he is! It turned out to be the turning point in all our lives, the beginning of a long road ahead. Was it good? In many ways, yes, because we finally got some answers about what was happening with him.

Somehow, a different pediatrician, an older man who was on sabbatical two years previously, had an idea about what could be causing David's issues. He ordered specific blood tests that had to be done in the States because they were not available in Canada at the time. I hope that has changed now for anyone else going through this. This doctor definitely thought outside the box. The test showed he had two rare conditions; one was called Kleinfelter's syndrome, a genetic, hormonal condition, which meant he had an extra female chromosome in his body. The other was Friedrich's Ataxia, a recessive genetic disorder, a debilitating disease with no cure. It was the reason he had lost his ability to walk. It attacks all the muscles in the body. I likened it to Multiple Sclerosis. I think these conditions also accounted for his behaviour issues, but there was nothing definitive to back that up at the time. Rare conditions are not studied as much as something more prevalent, which is why hardly anyone has heard of them and why there so few treatments. They can just manage the symptoms as they arise, which is what we did with David, but more about that later.

As of this writing, it is the first anniversary of David's passing. The word "anniversary" sounds strange to me; I feel it implies joy or a happy occasion. There are many anniversaries of sad and tragic things, so I guess there isn't another term. I hate the verb "was" instead of "is" and "used to" instead of "does." I avoid saying these, or I correct myself, so to speak. I find myself thinking I wish it were this time last year because David was here. It was the last time we watched a show together or listened to music. I always think of him when I see a certain show or hear a certain song. I suppose it's a way to try to stay connected to him. I ask him to make himself known or visible to me in a dream or when I'm awake, but I've not seen anything yet. I'll keep waiting. Anything is possible with God, right? I saw a medium with a friend who lost her mother a few months before David passed. I have never been to one before, but it was amazing! She knew things that she could never have known, like him not being well from a rare disorder. She said he wanted me to know that he had walked into the light. That is what people do, and she says that a lot, I imagine, but she said David was persistent about the fact that he "walked" into the light. I explained he had been in a wheelchair for most of his life. She also said that an elderly man who was very close to David as a child met him at the gate. The medium was also wearing an orange t-shirt, which I didn't notice until later. Orange was David's favourite colour. She said she usually wears a long sleeve shirt because she gets chills sometimes when she does her readings, but on this night, she was putting away her daughter's laundry and picked the orange t-shirt because it was a warm night. Everything sort of threw me. The last thing she said was that David told her it was time for me to take care of myself now. She couldn't have known he lived with us; I could have had him in a facility. It may seem strange, but I walked away feeling more at peace than I have in a long time.

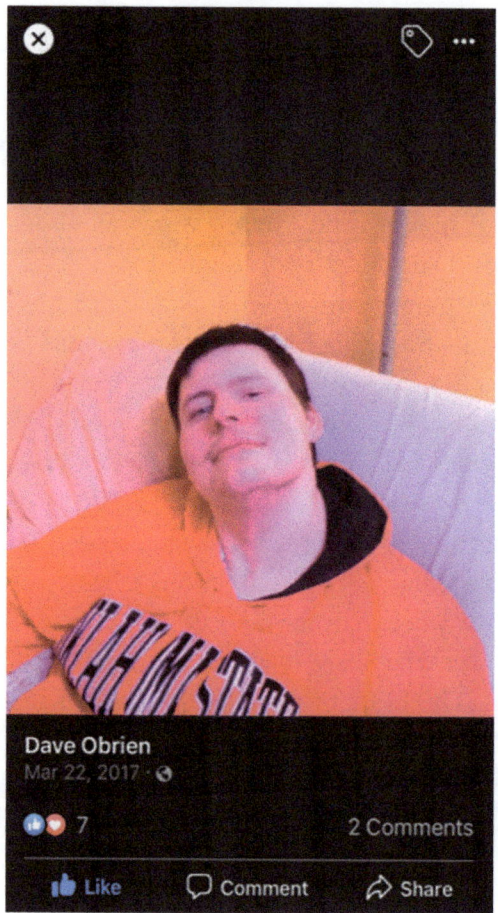

David wore orange as much as possible, he believed it would brighten people's day; as it did his.

My mom always says, "He's in a better place." How can it be a better place when I'm not with him? I feel selfish for wanting him back. I feel guilty for not being home when he needed me the most and for things that were beyond my control. I think this is normal, too; I don't know. Sometimes I think I should finally get some help; at least it would help me cope. I sometimes think what you believe has a lot to do with how you grieve. Religion plays a role in the grieving process; like mom said, a better place. We all know about heaven but not enough to ease the pain enough when you lose someone you love. My mom, a devout Catholic, believes heaven must exist; otherwise, what is the point of living your best life, following the commandments, and being kind and helpful to others? The reward is heaven; to meet up with loved ones you lost long ago, even your pets. That sounds wonderful! I hope that is the case for most of us. Good people "do unto others" and go to heaven and the worst of society go to the other place. That would be the fair thing to believe, that God gauges it that way, but where does forgiveness come in? If you lived a horrible life and did terrible things but sought forgiveness toward the end of your life, are you allowed in? My mom sometimes spoke of purgatory, the place you go when God doesn't know what to do with you. Being in limbo for eternity can't be pleasant! Who knows? I like to believe what my mom believes; it doesn't hurt to have a little faith in what might be in store for us if we live a life of love and kindness toward our fellow man. I like to think David is up in heaven with his grandpa, his cousin he lost a while back, and his childhood friend who left us too soon.

The feelings that wash over you and your random thoughts can feel strange if you can concentrate at all. I can't seem to keep a thought in my head for more than five seconds or finish a sentence. I find myself trailing off and not finishing my thoughts. I forget simple things, like the order of things and what I was doing or where I was going. It's very disconcerting! It's weird how it only feels like yesterday that you lost the person you loved because it's so raw and fresh, like a sudden cut to your hand. At other times, it feels like they've been gone forever because you miss them so much, and it runs so deep that you feel it in your soul! You worry about forgetting their laugh, voice, or smile. I try to remember that memories may fade in time, but the love will never fade. David made a few recordings of us talking mostly about the cats.

I treasure them and listen to them occasionally. For a few minutes, it's like he's in the room with me. I must get my mom on tape; it will be nice to hear her voice after she goes, which I hope isn't for a long time. I imagine that others hold onto phone messages and such because it helps.

Chapter 2

Our David was a very special person. People always say that about their loved ones, and it's always true. If you loved them, they were special! David had an enlarged heart, which was part of the Friedrich's, but his heart was also big emotionally. I recall him helping various people over the years, and he always put so much thought into everything he did. I say how he's an angel in heaven like he was one on earth. I would find him sitting, and he would say he was just "tinking," then the next day, he would do something extraordinary. When he was alone, which was a lot of the time, I thought he was bored or depressed, but it was rare for him to be down on himself or his circumstances. This was true throughout his life; if he got shot down by someone after trying to get one of his ideas to volition, he would stew for a bit and then come up with something else. He was a "lemonade out of lemons "kind of person.

When he loved you, he was always thinking about you—checking in on you, being helpful if he could, even to his detriment, like money. Sometimes he was too trusting, and others would take advantage. He always went above and beyond, especially with gifts. Birthdays and Christmas were special for him, not his but other people's. He would give others thoughtful gifts and what they needed or specifically wanted. His grandmother always loved Tweety from Tweety and Sylvester, so over the years, he bought her everything imaginable related to Tweety—placemats, slippers, a pendant watch, and a clock. Many times, Ray and I would be traipsing through the city because he found something online for Grandma Fuzz, as he called her, that he just had to get her. He always put a lot of thought into what he wanted to give someone. Some may say he went overboard, but my mom loved it, and he loved her. They always had a special bond. David was loved by his grandma in Newfoundland so much too. When he heard that her stereo wasn't working anymore, he took it upon himself to buy her a newer system with all the functions. He also mailed it to her; this was before Amazon, of course. She was elated and grateful to him that she always brought that up whenever David's name was mentioned. He knew she loved her music as he did. Later, he compiled quite a few CDs of Newfie songs and older country music that he looked up on the internet. David gave them to her when she came to visit one year, and she thought he was something else, and he was!

David's Grandma Fuzz, as he called her.

One time, he came home without his shirt on. It was a little late in the day and chilly out, so I was concerned. I asked what happened to his shirt, and he replied that he had seen a homeless man with a ratty old t-shirt, so he gave it to him. If you knew David and how he felt about his "chub," as he called it, you would know how significant this was. He hated anyone seeing his belly. He had to watch his weight since sitting in the wheelchair didn't allow him to exercise as much as he would have liked. I often wish he would have gotten into some wheelchair sports when they were offered years ago, but he always thought he would walk again, and that was it! David's weight gain was inevitable, and so was the diabetes diagnosis, which we knew was coming, as it was part of the Friedrich's ataxia. It is a brutal disease; just when you think you've had everything thrown at you, another decimating, tragic symptom knocks you down like pins in a bowling alley. I know all diseases are cruel in how they take away your abilities to walk, talk or especially think (dementia was a possibility for David), and then eventually take your life, unfortunately. Anyway, I was so proud of him, but that was him! I told him not to do that again because I was worried he would get sick. David didn't get sick too often, thank goodness, but when he did, he ended up with pneumonia a few times, which was very scary. The next day, he asked me to collect any old things he didn't wear or were too small so that he could take them to the person whom he gave his shirt. That was my boy; even with all his issues, he always looked out for someone else worse off. That started a whole new cause for him, and he was determined to help others however he could.

Some land around a gas station close to our home was up for sale for some time. David considered buying it and went to city hall to see who owned it. As it turned out, it was the Esso corporation. He also discovered that the land couldn't house storage containers that he wanted to retrofit for people to stay in because of zoning. He was heartbroken. He wanted to build cabins with bathrooms and showers for the homeless. Every day, he'd see more homeless people coming toward our end of town. It's ironic that as I'm writing this, we are in mid-July 2020, three months into the coronavirus pandemic. Going forward, I will not give the virus any more credence or power by capitalizing it. Due to the pandemic, the hotel I worked at was basically closed. Like most other businesses, it was extremely sad to watch, let alone be a part of; no one was travelling, of course. The hotel owners agreed to house some of the homeless from the House of Friendship downtown to keep them separated for safety from the virus. David would have been over the moon! For them to reside in those pricy rooms was quite the change for everyone.

Earlier this year, a woman who ran a convenience store downtown turned it into a haven for the homeless. Unfortunately, they had to leave because her neighbours didn't approve of her housing "those people." She later teamed up with a man who had a piece of land in a business district of the city and a gentleman who was a former city planner to make "a better tent city". On this lot of land, they built little cabins for them with doors that locked and gave the homeless keys.

Unfortunately, David never got to see this materialize. My mother says maybe somehow he inspired that gentleman that started this. I like to think so. He was always thinking of other people, partly to keep his mind off his troubles. He had a few on the horizon, unfortunately. We didn't talk about the future of his ailments unless it was staring us in the face. We had his tests done when needed, and we changed his medications when needed or added more. David disliked taking so many pills, but he did it for me, I think. I guess I looked worried most of the time. David's doctor officially retired a few years back but kept seeing David as a patient. He would come to the house when he had an issue or would just come to check in on him. He didn't really retire; he and his nurse started spending their days at St. John's Kitchen, a one-time homeless shelter downtown. It is more than that now; it's called The Working Center, which doesn't just house the homeless for a night or two and feed them; they help them find jobs and rooms or get an apartment someday. And because of this doctor, they had medical care. I imagine this wasn't easy at times; he told me once he had seen a lot of overdoses, unfortunately. Drugs were a part of these people's lives, but not all. I admire the people that see past all the stigma and do what they can to help. Dr. B. is an earth angel, which I've met a few of lately.

David started selling things online but not for money. He would ask for canned goods so that he could give them to the kitchen. He enjoyed trying to figure out how much something was worth in cans. This went on for months until I had to stop him from selling his personal things and ours. I was worried I would come home and not have a washer or TV. He would go down there and try to help, showing people computer skills or just talking and playing chess with them. David was very good. When his hands were still okay, he would play with Kyle; he even went to regionals for competitions and won a few awards when he was younger. He never got angry at losing control of his hands, not that I saw anyway; he basically took everything in stride, but he shouldn't have had to.

David's love of cars led to an obsession with learning to drive. We thought he put the idea of driving out of his mind, but it didn't go far. He loved cars and anything to do with them. For instance, he could tell you how to take apart a carburetor and put it back together. He was self-taught. He would watch car shows, fixer-upper shows, and every car video he could find. He could listen to the sound of a car and tell you what was wrong with it and how to fix it. One time, a neighbour couldn't get his motorbike to start. David, who was already in bed at the time, told me to tell him it was flooding, and he explained how to fix it. The neighbour did what David said, and it worked. They were surprised; David was always underestimated. Nobody would give him a chance. He tried multiple times to get a job at a dealership or a garage, even Canadian Tire, but all they saw was his wheelchair. He was hurt, of course, but not for long.

David's last car, an old Buick that he wanted to fix up

About six years ago, he found out that he needed to get a physical from the ministry of transportation to see if he could drive. He could only do it in London, Ontario, a fair distance from us. He got an appointment with the help of his occupational therapist. I wanted to go with him, but he made the appointment without my knowledge, and I couldn't take off work. I wanted him to do this to finally get a definitive answer on whether he could ever drive. In my heart, I knew he wouldn't be able to, but he had to hear it from someone in charge, especially from the government. I don't think he wanted me to go with him because I was always the voice of reason when he had his "dreams of grandeur," as described in his symptoms. In reality, I didn't want him to get physically or emotionally hurt. I didn't want him to get his hopes up when I knew they would not allow him to drive. At this point, his vision was also deteriorating; he had two different prescriptions in two years, and his hands were also becoming an issue. But he took the bus by himself and went anyway. Unfortunately, his appointment got pushed to the next day, so he was stuck at the London hospital. Fortunately, a nurse called to tell me she would take care of him. She and her paramedic boyfriend brought him to a motel, gave him something to eat, and then brought him back to the hospital the next day for his appointment. He was prepared to sleep in his chair at the hospital. I was floored by their kindness. Unfortunately, David's appointment didn't go well, and they told him he couldn't drive. I was beside myself with worry, but the nurse said he was fine but devastated that he couldn't get his license. I think he knew deep down, but he had to exhaust all possibilities. He was in a funk for a while until his next venture—a car lot for people who couldn't afford much!

As I write this, the second anniversary of his passing is upon us. I'm going to stop calling it an anniversary; instead, I will call it David's Memorial Day! I still find it so hard to believe he's gone. David's friend Rose, whom he wanted to call his girlfriend, wanted a few of his stuffed animals, which he called "the family." They were good company for him. He had some since he was a baby. He spent too much time in his room, which I didn't like, but he seemed at peace doing so. Anyway, I gave her a big teddy bear that he had from mom that he called Kyle Bear 2 and a bunny he got one Easter. I have a picture of him hugging the bear on my phone. I cherish it. He also had a raccoon called Randy and a country bear called Tyler he had since childhood. There were others, like a little teddy with a heart that said "To the One I Love" that he got for Valentine's Day from his grandma and a lamb and duck he got at different Easters. He was sentimental that way. He took a lot of solace in having them around. They weren't hidden by any means; they were always on his bed, and he slept with a different one each night. The most prominent one was a big, fluffy black-and-white cow he got from his grandma. Did I mention he loved cows too? Her name is Bessie, and from what I ascertain, she's around seventy years old and very contrary. David started talking to her, and for her, and I eventually did too! All this may sound childish, but it gave him comfort and that was important. I have them in my room now, and I sleep with a different one each night too. It gives me a little comfort. He had a little orange bunny called Creamsicle that I got him for Easter. I put her in his coffin with him for company so that he wasn't alone. David loved the three "C's"— cars, cats, and cows. Speaking of cows, one of David's first encounters with one was when we went to Prince Edward Island the year the Confederation bridge opened. We decided to spend some time there, on our way to Newfoundland to see Ray's family to find the small town where my dad grew up in P.E.I. There were different farms all around, and if he wasn't in sight, we knew where he was—with the moos. I was concerned because I had heard they can be unpredictable, but they were fast friends, and he never forgot about hanging out with them. We ended up getting a cottage down the road from the Anne of Green Gables house. It was such a wonderful trip for David and us. He loved playing on the beach and climbing on the clay cliffs of the shore. That was the last summer he could walk. I'm so glad he had those memories to hang onto, and Ray and I also.

David with his Kyle Bear, named after his brother.

Our cat Shy with some of David's other moos.

His friend Rose wondered why I still had his bed and wheelchair and why his room was still intact. I only had given away his clothes to the men's hostel that his doctor worked at, and that was after he passed. Winter was coming, and I know he would have wanted them to be used by someone who needed them. The chair had to remain because of the two-year limit to do something legally about his death. I was expecting the wheelchair company to come and get it because the government partly paid for it. David passed away partly because the company that put in his chest straps didn't finish their job. They cancelled two appointments with me, his PSWs, and his occupational therapist to show us how to use them safely and where they went on his body—that is so important! Ray found him almost on the floor against a wall and not breathing. He did CPR on him and got his heart going, and called 911. They came, and his poor heart went down at least five more times between our home and the hospital. When they did an MRI, they couldn't find any brain activity from the lack of oxygen. It stands to reason that if the chest straps were in place and his heart gave out, which is what we think happened, his head would have dropped to the side or forward. How horrifying for Ray and Kyle. I found out later that Kyle was down there also because they came in the front and woke him. David's room was in the basement, and there was a laneway at the back with access to the basement. I guess Ray, in his distress, didn't mention to the paramedics to go to the back. Ray had him back at that point, his heart anyway, and David was still unconscious. The doctors said there wasn't any way for him to come back to us; he had brain damage. They didn't expect him to wake up. We could have put him up in a room and prolonged things, but after sitting with him for a few hours and remembering what he went through over the course of the day, the pain he was constantly in, and what lay ahead, I made the toughest decision of my life. His poor, loving, giving heart wouldn't sustain him any longer. I know he wouldn't have wanted to be incapacitated. We discussed it a few times; we weren't maudlin about it, but I knew how he felt, and I couldn't put him through that. I say I because Ray and Kyle didn't want to say anything. After all, they knew I would do what I wanted. It would have been nice to share in the decision; I still feel strange about that. I guess that's how it is in some families; one person usually makes the main decisions, and in ours, that was me. One thing we did agree on was that he needed to rest.

David had a lot of ailments, but he still wanted to give what he could. He ended up giving his corneas to the Trillium Gift of Life program. He wanted to do this when he got his license, or beginners in his case, which was as far as he got, unfortunately. We talked about signing the back of the license and how important it is to donate your organs, tissue, etc. If he could have given anything else, he would have, but with everything he had wrong with him, he couldn't; there were strict guidelines. I hope whoever got his corneas has the type of vision David had for life and helping people. The horror of it all was so unnecessary. If they followed through with what they were supposed to do, things wouldn't have been so traumatic for him, Ray, and Kyle. Of course, it would have been better if he had just passed in his sleep, which is how everyone wants to go, but for him, it really would have been better. I know people die in terrible circumstances every day, which is traumatic for all their loved ones, but in our world, it was our dear David!

I reached out to several lawyers who all said they couldn't start a case for negligence or wrongful death because I chose not to do an autopsy. I didn't remember being asked, but Ray said I had said no because I thought he had been through enough, which he had! I know it made no sense, but the situation was far from rational. Oh, God, my poor boy! I could just scream sometimes! It's so awful! Later, I heard that when people die at home or incidents occur at home, an autopsy is usually required by law. I wish they would have insisted in this case and taken it out of my hands, knowing what I know now. I guess they were just trying to honour my wishes after what he had been through and because of all his ailments. So, they listed his cause of death as heart failure. I sometimes think there is a reason it happened this way: his death could mean change for other people with disabilities. His big heart, in all senses of the word, failed him, which we always knew was a possibility. For it to be exacerbated by a simple thing like an appointment being kept is mind-boggling and very disturbing.

We miss him so much; he was such a constant in our lives! The emptiness, loss, and loneliness are so profound that it's almost too much to bear at times. I feel that if it weren't for my mom, Ray, and Kyle, I would choose to join him. Waking up each day is torture, knowing he's not here! I know why people give up on life after losing someone they love so dearly; it is just the worst. I feel like I just want to get through the rest of my life. After all, family and love are the most important things in life, aren't they?

I hope I can come to some peace of mind and reconcile all this. My niece once said that we were so close because we basically grew up together. I guess we did. In the purest sense, he was my first love, the one person you care about more than anything. Each day brings new memories back to me; either I cry or laugh or just stare at the sky and talk to him about what I'm thinking. That's one of the things I miss the most—the conversations we would have. We could tell each other anything. Sometimes he would keep something from me that he was planning but not for long because his excitement would take over or he was looking for some validation, which I usually gave but cautiously. He never saw himself as disabled or different; he just expected to do what others did, but differently. He was amazing in every way!

Chapter 3

There are different kinds of people in this world, and David encountered all of them. You have those who would pull over in their car and take a half-hour to push his chair out of a snowy ditch in freezing temperatures and follow him home to ensure he got there okay. Then you have those who just drove by. David would get himself into predicaments like that countless times. He depended on the kindness of strangers, and I am pleased to say that most of the time, it paid off! He would even drive through the trails, which scared me to no end, as I always worried about him getting robbed or worse. Some people can be so cruel. Most people were just indifferent and ignored him, which made him angry, so he would do something to get in their faces, like purposely bumping into them. He knew better, but with the Klinefelter's, his maturity level wasn't always what it should have been. He just wanted respect like everyone else! He met a lot of ignorant people, ignorant in every sense of the word. David sometimes felt bad about himself and even wrote on his social media profile: "I am a person, believe it or not!" When I read that, I bawled. To be ignored by your peers and strangers must be hard to reconcile. When he got older, he was better at ignoring things, but in high school, he got in trouble a few times, which I think stemmed from being ostracized. No one likes being made to look like an idiot, or worse, have no friends.

I recently came across some old paperwork from the University of Waterloo. They wanted to study David because he was the recipient of two rare disorders. I agreed because I thought it would help him deal with his issues. He also agreed. I wouldn't have done it otherwise. He thought it was cool. He was in his teens, and his hormones had gone awry, but for him, it was amplified because his were compromised as it were. I hope they got some insight into his disorders to one day help others with them. I also found some pertaining to David's high school years. He began these years with a lot of upheaval in his life. His beloved grandfather passed away, his first death, and he no longer had his teacher's assistant with whom he had bonded in grade school. Adjusting wasn't easy for him, to say the least. The school was on the other side of the city, but they picked it because it had an elevator. When I was reading this old paperwork, I got so upset because I had forgotten how bad it got back then. The school had two young men as teacher's assistants; over time, he found common interests with them, and one of those interests was music. They had a band, and, of course, David thrived on music. He was good for periods of time, but when he was around other students for any length of time, the you-know- what hit the fan! The reports said he made rude comments like, "Is that what you're wearing to go downtown tonight?" I am sure he was provoked, but even a dismissive glance from a girl, especially if he liked her, could cause him to say something cruel and hurtful, especially if that's how they made him feel.

He made a few friends, mostly just guys that wanted something from him, but he knew that, and he didn't care. He would just make a deal with them for something he wanted in return. When David was at this school, computers were still new. David was very underestimated as far as understanding and working on them, and we got one shortly after they came out. He would help people with his computer skills in exchange for watching his back when he would get bullied. He ended up getting suspended several times for breaking the firewall on the library computer. He was super smart, but all everyone saw was his wheelchair. Things got worse as the years went on. I was almost at the end of grade ten that he had a big blow-up. I can't remember what set him off, but he was told to go home. They called his wheelchair van, but he didn't want to go. He got so angry that he went down the street to a grocery store and started knocking things off the shelves. He had bursts of anger but taking it out on the store was the most impulsive he had ever been. I think the school did their best, but looking back, they had no idea how to deal with someone like David. Physical disabilities are almost easier to deal with than emotional or psychological ones. These days, behavioural issues are more prevalent and studied.

That was his last day at school. Several teachers followed him that day, not his TAs, which would have been better, and proceeded to restrain him physically. I guess this went on for a bit. In the meantime, they called Ray to come to the plaza. He lost it and almost decked one of the teachers when he saw how he was restraining David. Ray talked David into coming home; he always had a way with him. He loved him, and no matter the conflict, Ray was there for him. Ray was so angry, more than I'd ever seen him. As I said, I don't recall how things shook out that day, but David was a lot happier not having to go there every day. Later, David tried homeschooling on the computer, but that didn't last long because he found it hard to concentrate. If it were something he was interested in, it would have been different, just like the rest of us.

David stayed at home playing games on the Nintendo and computer. As time passed, the neighbours all knew him, and he was very well-liked. He seemed to come to terms with being in his chair and different. It was a long road for us; it wasn't easy to reconcile, especially for him. "Reconcile" is a loaded word I'm finding out. Years before, we were involved with the local rotary centre for kids with disabilities. They offered things like horseback riding, sledge hockey, and other activities. David flatly refused! He was not like them; he would get better and be normal again! Unfortunately, that was not to be. It made fitting him for his new wheelchair challenging, but we managed. He didn't like going there at all, but he knew he was losing his ability to walk. It was an internal struggle of immense proportion, and I admire him when I look back. He was stubborn in many ways, but at the same time, he seemed to go along with things. It must have been so hard at his age, not to mention frightening. So, when he turned a corner, it was a relief. He would go to the store for people, help watch over the younger children, and, of course, his favourite, helping with car repairs. I was thinking about the times we were apart, and I only remember one time. When Kyle was still in grade school, David would sometimes take him to school for me. One day, on his way home, he was hit by an idiot in a van backing out of his driveway. The man took off! Luckily, a bus came by, and the driver stopped to help. David was taken to the hospital and discovered his tibia was broken in two places. It was horrible. It set him back physically, not to mention it was painful. David could tolerate a lot, but this was another level. I couldn't take care of him; with the stronger medications he needed, the doctor thought it was best to put him in a nursing home for six weeks while he healed. I reluctantly agreed. He healed quickly, which amazed us, and he had a good time in there. He bought pizza and chicken for the residents and played cards and chess with them, but mostly, he listened to their life stories, especially if they were in one of the wars. David loved history. He made something tragic that happened to him as good as possible. That was him!

A couple of years ago, about six months before David passed, a girl who lived down the street started at work. When we were on break one day, and I spoke to her about David, as I often did, she put it together that David was the same young man who would help her with her kids and give them rides on his chair. I wasn't fuzzy with that part, but she didn't seem to mind. It was nice to hear someone tell me how sweet, kind, and gentle he was because that's how I knew him. She has turned into one of my best friends. It's unfortunate that David never got together with us and shared those memories because all this unfolded a week before he died. She often tells me different stories about David's interactions with her kids, which helps. Talking about the person you lost is a way of keeping their memory alive and making your heart hurt just a little less. You're grateful! During his times around the neighbourhood, he met a nice older gentleman down the street who ran a TV and radio repair shop out of his garage. David would pick up any electronics he would see at the side of the road and take them to this man, "the boss," as he would call him. The man would fix them up and resell them, and he would give David pocket money. His bond with this man was phenomenal; he was like a grandfather to him. David met him a couple of years after my dad passed away. David missed that in his life, I think. This man would later put a stereo on the back of David's chair, and David would go up and down the street, playing his beloved AC/DC. David would call him for advice occasionally, and I think a third opinion on something he was planning was very helpful. He was a special man, and it hit him hard when David passed. I wish I had checked in on him, but unfortunately, he passed a year later. I'm sure David looked him up in heaven.

This sales aspect of David's life became his goal and opened a whole new endeavour for him. He had what it took. I think he could sell anything to anybody! Since cars were his passion, he didn't want to give that up. He started buying cars or trucks from the newspaper or online, knowing we didn't have the space to store them, but that didn't stop him. He would store them at my mother's or the neighbour's. We had one or two here for a while until the landlord caught on. Everyone tried to accommodate him for a while anyway. Ray would do what he could to do minor repairs with David's help, but it got to the point where it had to stop. He bought cars at an auction with the help of his friend, who had a tow truck with a flatbed, and he would bring them wherever David could store them. He met all kinds of people over those years. Some men would come here with a part or two that David would buy for one of his cars. Sometimes he got ripped off; other times, he would get a good deal on something. Like with other things in his life, some people would take advantage of him, but he learned from all of it. I think he mostly enjoyed people coming to the house to talk about cars with him and Ray. David finally gave that up when his friend with the tow truck never paid back a loan he had given him. This so-called friend also had a junk yard and sold some cars, and David would hang out there sometimes and help people look for things in the yard. David bought a few of them, thinking he could fix them up and sell them for more, but the guy ended up charging him too much to store them there, so David wasn't making anything. I think if he had just tried to work with David and given him a commission for sales, it would have worked out great for them both. But he was too selfish for that, and David was let down again. To make matters worse, David had loaned him the money to pay off a debt, and this guy claimed that David used all the money on tows from long ago. It wasn't true; David kept records of everything. We tried to get it back from him, but he wasn't budging. David thought about taking him to court, but we decided it wasn't worth it. All I know is there is a special place in hell for people who take advantage of others, disabled or not. I'm sure this was the catalyst for "DCOB Car Sales," he would run a fair car lot.

    Later, with cars still on his mind, saving up to open his own, David tried to get jobs at different dealerships but to no avail. To be a car salesperson, you must drive. He was crushed again! I wish they could have hired him to be a greeter so that he could have talked cars with people while waiting for their oil changes, for example. He would have loved that! I wanted him to try a parts place. With his knowledge, it would have been a great fit, but he didn't want to be behind a counter; he wanted to be in a garage or a lot. I have never seen anyone persevere as much as him. I was so proud of him. Later, when he wanted to get his own car lot going, he checked into getting his credentials. The Ontario Motor Vehicle Industry Council regulates sales of vehicles to protect the consumer, things like price gouging and fair and honest competition from dealers. David studied his huge heart off, and I helped him by quizzing him. I was so proud of him, and he was proud of himself, too, I could tell. He planned to take his test orally at the library in town with one of the school's representatives. He did well; I think he got 80 percent. He accomplished this a couple of years before he passed, which is sad because he never got to show the naysayers that he could do what they did.

I'm writing this in stages like most writers, I guess, but with me, it's taking a lot longer. As you can imagine, it's very hard at times. When I get going, I can get on a roll, but getting to that point has an aura of dread. That sounds strange as I am writing about him but dealing with his loss daily or minute by minute basis. It is daunting. Sitting down intentionally and remembering our story and his life is hard. It is sometimes a bit helpful but painful at others, so please bear with me. I find myself crying or smiling at memories of certain TV shows like *The Flintstones*, or a certain phrase like "Yabba Dabba Do means I love you" or "Let the sunshine in," the song Pebbles and Bam Bam sang. David loved all the old shows like *MASH*, *Golden Girls*, and *All in the Family*. I would sing the opening song and do Edith's screech, and David would howl; he loved it! Now when I catch a glimpse of those shows or hear a theme song, I'm taken back there. Emotionally, it's tough to remember. I think to myself that David was here the last time I saw that or heard that. At times, David didn't have too much to fill in his days, so he became invested in his TV shows. He liked a variety of shows, mostly comedies like *The Simpsons* and *Family Guy*. He thought Seth MacFarlane was the greatest since the Chevy. He loved *Dumb and Dumber* most of all. He liked all Jim Carey movies, but that was his favourite. Tom Hanks was also a favourite, and he would always watch *Forest Gump*. I think he identified with misunderstood and ostracized characters. He once taped the part of *Dumb and Dumber* that the character Harry had in the bathroom after Lloyd put a huge amount of laxative in his drink. He had this hilarious and rude exclamation on his phone as a voicemail message. He would do anything for a laugh. He loved laughing, and I loved hearing him laugh, as the rest of his life left something to be desired. Any enjoyment was so welcome to him. David had a tremendous laugh; it would start slow, then off he would go! On the other side, he loved movies like *The Fugitive, The Untouchables, Shawshank Redemption,* and a movie I can't bring myself to watch, *Payback 1999*. He found it and put it on YouTube. I still have his phone, and he gets emails from people who agree with him that it was a great movie. This warms my heart. I haven't cancelled his Facebook, YouTube, or email. I think many people leave that stuff active for a while, and there is nothing wrong with that. Cancelling would have a finality about it, as though they are really gone—it's too tough.

After he passed, I would look up at the sky more often. I had also heard that from other people. I would see a beautiful orange sunset and think David painted it. I would find heart-shaped chips and cherries and think they were signs from him. I know it sounds silly, but it gave me some peace. I'm past the bartering stage of wanting to bring him back. It wouldn't be fair to bring him back so he could suffer all his ails again. But if he could come back healthy? I often think of where and who he'd be if he wasn't so unfortunate, medically. He was rare in so many ways; I'm only touching on a few, but I think he was who he was in a way because of how he was. I believe he would have still been the kind and compassionate person he was if he wasn't disabled and grew up to drive, have a relationship, a job he loved, and later a family, but maybe not to the extent he was. Because of how he was, he took a lot of time and forethought in everything he did. When you have a lot of things going on in your life, it's tough to go out of your way for people like he did. We all want to be more charitable and giving in our lives, but let's face it, the average person doesn't have the time for that. Our trials and tribulations in life shape us in ways we may never understand. He was in unfortunate circumstances physically and emotionally, so it gave him insight into others of equal or similar situations, the most vulnerable and marginalized people. It's easier to understand each other when we see our similarities instead of differences. David did that every day or at least tried to when people would give him a chance, which wasn't very often, unfortunately. When I see orange, his favourite colour, I believe it reflects who he was—strong, bright, and beautiful! He got his Daddy Fuzz, as he called Ray, to paint his room orange. He had orange shirts, coats, sheets, and blankets. Even the decals and controller golf ball on his chair were orange; it was never too much. Yes, he went a little overboard with that too, but there are worse things to be obsessed with. As I've mentioned, David's love for AC/DC was immeasurable; they were his favourite band. He knew everything about them, had lots of memorabilia, sang the songs, and could tell you how Bon Scott died, where they live, etc. When they came for the Toronto SARS concert in 2003, he had to go. We had been to a few of their concerts together before, but I couldn't attend this one because Kyle was small and Ray was working. So, he went by himself on the bus. I was worried, but there was no stopping him. He was still good then as far as his hands and upper body was concerned. I knew there would be help if he needed it, and I couldn't stop him if I wanted to. When he set his sights on something, he had to follow through. Every time AC/

DC came, David was there. AC/DC gave him a lot of joy. People say music is an escape; for David, that was so true.

**One of many beautiful orange sunsets
I take the time to notice now.**

A few months after he passed, I wanted to have a celebration of life for him, but I wanted to make it a giving benefit to keep his giving spirit alive. I came across this lady on social media who had started a cat rescue out of her home. It has expanded now, and she has a facility close to downtown. She rescues feral stray cats in colonies, has them fixed and looked at by a vet, then releases them back to their colony. Those that are alone or mothers and babies are checked out, treated, spayed and neutered, and put up for adoption. It's truly terrible how some people treat animals. Our city has a terrible stray cat problem, and my friend is trying to help them; she is truly an earth angel. David would have loved her. I picture him volunteering at her facility, being the official "petter and hugger." When I had the idea for the benefit concert, I knew she had to be a part of it. I also wanted the Working Centre to be a part of it. David always tried to help that place and the people, as his doctor did. I hired an AC/DC cover band, booked a venue, got tickets printed, ordered catering, bought prizes for a raffle, and my friend brought auction items. It was hard to pin down a date, but we did it in the summer. It was a great time, and we raised two thousand dollars for the cat rescue and the working centre, but mostly, it was a chance to be together doing what David loved to do—listen to AC/DC. I know he was there with us, rocking along.

The picture of the poster from the concert.

As I'm writing, another birthday of mine is upon me, Mama Fuzz, as David called me. Anyone or anything he loved was fuzzy and orange, of course. I still hear "Mama fuzz," said with such exuberance, which still brings a tear to my eye. Walking out the door and going to work that morning was the last time I talked to him and saw him alive. I look over and picture him there, smiling whenever I walk out the door. I still can't believe it to this day; how can someone be here one day and not the next, or one hour and not the next, for that matter? It is unfathomable to me. I must believe he is here with us, watching over us. It helps to get me through the rough days, of which there are still so many. I try to think of things the way David always did. He was always upbeat, knew how to look beneath the surface for many things, and didn't want to give up on anything; there was always a way. It was his life's motto and code. Oh, my love! I miss you so much. Other times, I don't know how I get through; it may sound strange, but I've gotten used to saying, "another day has gone by without you, another tomorrow, and I'm that much closer to seeing you again," at the end of each day.

Grief is a burden you bear when you lose someone you love, but it becomes almost unbearable when it comes with regret. I wish I had never gone to work that day. I was supposed to be off, but I went in because, ironically, my co-worker had to go to a funeral. I told my mom that I should have been home, but she said you weren't meant to be. Maybe I would have had a heart attack or fainted. I don't think I would have because I would have gotten him on his bed earlier in the day, and he wouldn't have ended up in that horrendous position. I can't even remember if I kissed him goodbye that morning, but I must have because I usually did, but I keep second-guessing myself because it's so important. I know we talked because he wanted Chinese food for supper. He wanted it the night before, but I was home that day from work. I told him I would get it for supper that night. He loved Chinese food; it was his favourite. I wish I would have gotten it for him for his last night. God, that is horrible even to write! It just shows that you should never put things off, even for a day, because you never know what can happen to you or your loved ones. I remember that last morning and look at the empty bed since then and wish he was still there. We would get through whatever life had in store for him like we always did. Is that selfish? It is, but I know he didn't want to go yet, either. Besides, I'm his mom; I should never have had to say goodbye to him that way or any other.

Chapter 4

I still think about what might have been if I had put him up in a room for a week or so to see if he would come out of it. Would weeks have turned into months, wishing he would regain some consciousness, praying for a miracle? You never know; miracles happen, so why couldn't he have one? As I said, I'm second-guessing myself. I remember saying to my neighbour that we should move after he passed. I couldn't fathom being around his things, seeing him everywhere, hearing his laugh in my head. He said, "You'd regret that!" He was right; we would have. It's hard at first, but everything is, but you have a sense of solace being where he was and around his things. I sit in his orange room a lot, talking to him. At one point, for a lot of years, David had dinkey cars still packaged all over his walls. He got Ray to put nails all around the top part of every wall. He would add to them every time he went shopping; it gave him a lot of pleasure. When he passed, I gathered quite a few of them and set them up on a table at the funeral home. Everyone got to choose a keepsake of something David loved. I thought he would've approved. David also had a corkboard on his wall with pictures of his friend and cousin who had passed, the cats, and Kyle, so I added pictures of him at different ages. It's nice to look at; it's like a memory board. I sit, cry, and pray mostly for him to come home for a minute so that I can see and talk to him. I keep thinking he might be angry with me either for not being there for him that day or for letting him go instead of giving him a chance to fight back. I know it's not healthy, but that is how I feel at present. I know in my heart of hearts that he wouldn't blame me. Did he know he was going downhill as fast as he was? I listen to some recordings he had made a little while before he passed, and I can hear his laboured breathing and slower speech. It is very hard to listen to, but I cherish it.

I bought some strings of orange lights to put around his room. He already had lights up to help him see at night to pee, which he did in a bottle. I just wanted some orange ones up. I wish I had done that a long time ago! We get busy with our day-to-day lives and let the little things go that are just as important. The lights gave his room a warm and cozy feeling. I also bought some for the window in our living room, and I turn them on at night. I like to think he might look down and see them and know we're thinking of him. Wouldn't that be nice if our loved ones could peek through the clouds at us? Is that goofy? I don't care! We also put a battery-operated candle on the balcony when it gets dark. I also have one in a lantern at his stone in the cemetery. His stone was something to think about, but the gentleman there was very good. He asked us about David, what he liked to do, and what kind of person he was. Arrangements are hard to do, especially so suddenly, which is how David passed, but he made it a little easier. We ended up with a picture of a 1969 Chevy and a cat playing with a ball. The artist who drew the car was terrific and asked us our opinion throughout the process. Luckily, it got put in before the snow came that year. Apparently, if it's after, you have to wait until spring. I don't think I would have liked not having his marker there. I feel bad for the folks who must wait, but they allow you to put up a wooden cross at the site, which is wonderful for the time being; they never used to do that.

David's Heart

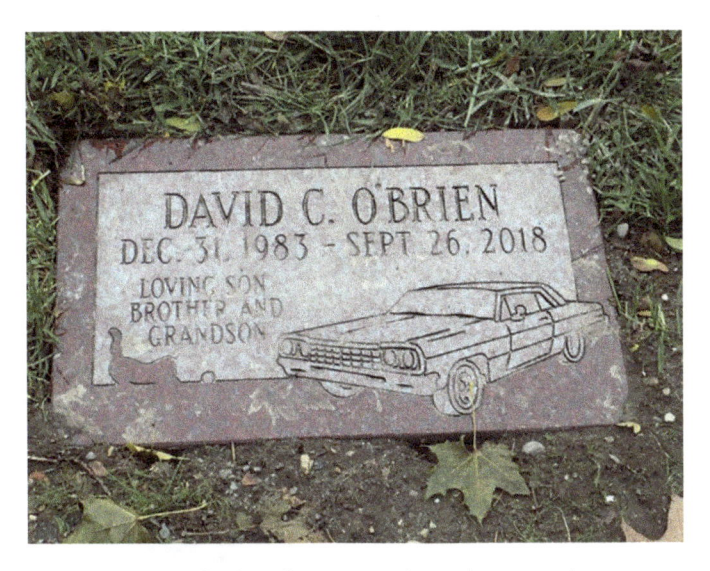

**David's headstone with a Chevy and
a cat. I'm sure he approves.**

 When I go upstairs in the evening, I light a candle in front of a picture of him and the one in the tall glass picture candle the funeral home gave me. I think I've only missed lighting them once or twice when I wasn't feeling well and went right to bed. It feels important to me to do this; it symbolizes that he was one of the lights in our lives. I put on a little tea light in front of his pictures upstairs and downstairs overnight. I don't know; it gives me some peace. For the first year or so, I would still look at the clock to see if it were 9:30— the time I would give him his fruit. Getting out of routines you've done for so long takes a while. Every little thing I can't do for him anymore is like a stab in my heart. It's unbelievable how your person not being here impacts even the most minor things in your life. I still can't believe it sometimes. I half expect him to be sitting in his chair or on his bed, smiling at me when I go downstairs. I talk to him all the time; that will never change. It breaks my heart that he cannot answer me or that we can't laugh together, which we always did. Missing him doesn't seem like a strong enough word.

The candle from the funeral home I light every night.

We still have his wheelchair; the damn vendor never came for it. I was told they would since the government paid for it. Now that it's over five years old, I'm told they don't want it back. I guess we will try to sell it. Someone might as well be using it. It was fitted for David, but that can be easily changed. I think they think they might be opening a can of worms if they get in touch with us. What can they say? There is nothing to say. They did not take any responsibility for anything that happened; they didn't even acknowledge they missed appointments. I had gotten a weak condolence email when I got in touch with them. They told me David was hard to please and very hard on his chair. WOW! What a way to talk to a parent whose child died partly by your negligence. Appalling; I still can't believe it. The arrogance!

Ray said he'd rather throw it off a bridge or run it over with the truck. I can't imagine what he lives with daily, finding David like that and trying to help him. He did what he could, and I hope he knows that; I certainly told him so. We know where the blame lies. I'm not saying David wouldn't have died, but it wouldn't have been under those horrific circumstances. He still had things to do, places to go, and music to listen to! Every lawyer I talked to, and there were quite a few, said they couldn't prove neglect or anything else because we didn't have an autopsy. I think they could have tried because there are records of cancelled appointments and a witness, David's occupational therapist. I don't know; maybe it would have been too much, but I would have liked to have been able to try. Justice for David is the ongoing goal; I will not stop until that place has been taken to task and the badly needed oversight is in place. In the meantime, there his wheelchair sits as a constant reminder of the horrific ordeal. I have other avenues I'm considering to try to change things for people with disabilities. I definitely do not want any other person to go through what we have.

I've considered other agencies to try to hold them accountable in some way, like ADP—the Assisted Devices Program for Ontario. They help finance devices for people and are the brokers between the public and the vendors, or I should say "vendor," since they monopolize the industry. That's one way to get all the business: no competition or oversight; you can do what you want. I later found out that they have a contract with the government. I imagine it's like the cities; different companies bidding for the jobs. There are questionable practices regarding the sale of parts and charges for labour. As of now, a member of parliament has told me that they are being investigated by the auditor general—good! David kept all his receipts and invoices in case we needed them, and he even called and got copies of anything he didn't have. My smart young man! We dealt with a few other places, like I said, a main big chain one, but suddenly, they didn't deal with the chairs anymore, and now we know why! I'm sure this new vendor is crooked, and the government is oblivious. Very frightening!

With covid still a real threat everywhere as I'm writing this, the nursing homes are in the news because of the lack of oversight and atrocious conditions. How these vulnerable people, our older generation, have been treated is unbelievable. Sadly, it took a pandemic to bring all these terrible circumstances to the forefront, much to our collective disgust. Not that the nurses and PSWs haven't tried before, but like with many other things, the government didn't listen. Shining a light on something can bring about change, but this is such a huge problem that was inherited from the former government, so it will take years to rectify. If people are on a fixed income, they are put into overcrowded places, which means there is less care for everyone. My mom was fortunate to have her house money to fall back on, and she is in one of the nicer places in town. How does this tie in with our David? Many family members told me to put him in a facility several times over the years. I didn't want to do that, even before I knew what they were like, and when I found out, I was so grateful and blessed that we could have our dear boy home with us for as long as we did. It was challenging at times, but we got help when we needed it, and he thrived, which I know for a fact that he wouldn't have done in a government-run home. It would have broken his spirit! Anyway, the same can be said for this wheelchair place; nobody is looking after the practices of this place, and it is unconscionable, especially when they deal with our most vulnerable citizens. It is shameful and disgraceful, especially today! So, ADP was no help to me because what I was asking didn't exist yet!

Weeks have passed, and I sometimes find it hard to write, as I mentioned before. It's almost like I do everything in my power to avoid it! I talked with an MPP in Ottawa that heard about me from an MPP in my city. I have written anyone and everyone I can think of. The MPP in Ottawa has an emphasis on helping people with disabilities and seniors, and he was very sympathetic to David's story and what we've been through since. He has a podcast I did a while ago, and they are writing an official letter to the vendor about the terrible care and service and their response to David's death or lack thereof. He also spoke about David in the legislature, which has given me a sense of hope that I'm finally getting somewhere, and I am so grateful that David's name will be on the record for all time. I also started a petition around that time on change.org., but it's slow going; I hope it will gain some momentum. We will see! Something has to work; David couldn't have died in vain.

Going to the cemetery each week helps a bit, it also reminds you of the loss, but it's important. I bought a new string with orange leaves covering the light. David loved fall, especially for the colours—the more orange, the better, of course. You can't help but feel cheated, and so is anyone who knew him or strangers he hadn't met yet. Sad! He couldn't do much toward the end, but to have his life cut short because someone couldn't be bothered to come back and finish their job is cruel, unnecessary, and frankly criminal, in my opinion. I'm just incensed! I don't know what I would do if I ran into the lady that worked for the vendor who had cancelled our appointments. It's just so hard to reconcile. Sometimes I feel like I'm living outside my body, watching it happen to someone else's family, which very well could be! I sometimes get so lonely that I want to join him. I know that I'm not unique to those feelings; other people have felt the same, especially after a profound loss. Feeling lonely even when you're around other people when someone so special to you is gone is normal; it's hard not to feel anything but despair. I sit on his bed and talk to him and cry so much that I get a headache, but it alleviates the heaviness in my chest. I miss our conversations so much; we would talk about the silliest things sometimes. There are times I wish my faith was stronger so that I would be more at peace with him being at peace up there. I guess thinking he is up there with God and his grandpa alludes to a certain amount of faith. I remember being at the mass at our church for all those who died that year. I went with my mom, who always sits in the first section on the right, close to the door. There was also an alcove with statues and candles to light to the right of us. During the mass, a little statue fell on the floor, and everyone was startled, even the priest. It was a windy night, so most chalked it up to the draft in the church, but then the snuffer stick fell to the floor when the names of the departed were being read aloud. I can't recall where David's name was in relation to the well-timed, strange occurrence, but I felt that our loved ones were letting us know they were there with us. It was strange but in a good way, and there wasn't anyone else around at the time. Maybe it's just a case of believing what I want but maybe it isn't. How something like that can help you is the main thing, and it did!

I've been off work for over a year now. Friday, March 13th, was my last day last year—ironic or what? As I probably mentioned, David always wanted me to be at home with him. I should have considered getting a caregiver's allowance but knowing the government, it wouldn't have been that much. I would have been at home with him that day—oh my, could have, would have, should have! So many euphemisms, and so much injustice in the world, especially this past year. It's been terrible, but you don't pay attention unless it directly hits you or your family. When we see something bad on TV, we think, "Oh my, that's awful," then we change the channel or scroll up on our phones. A story comes up in a faraway country, and we think, "Oh well, that doesn't affect me." We put it out of our minds because it's too hard to think about until it happens to your family. How we deal with things is shaped by our history and different experiences. Our perceptions of these experiences impact how we react to everything in our lives. I was telling my sister how on the day David was taken to the hospital, I was at work, and Ray called and told me what happened. He came to get me, and I went home and showered because I was sticky from work; it was a particularly hot September day. I thought what happened to David was the usual – a new prescription for his heart was needed – and that I would be stuck waiting at the hospital for hours, sweaty and uncomfortable. My sister said I was being practical. I don't know; I honestly thought this was one of those times. Ray didn't tell me differently, but I guess he didn't know how. I even brought David's phone and Bessie, his favourite moo, in the truck. I didn't end up bringing them up, but I should have brought Bessie at least; he might have sensed she was there if he touched her. All Ray said about his phone was, "I don't think he'll need that for a while," and that was the first time he let on that it was worse than I thought.

Being there felt like an hour, but it was almost three by the time we left the house and after seven when we got home. Looking back, I feel terrible because we left him before he was really gone. How could I have done that? It later dawned on me that he had to remain alive so that they could get his corneas, which he was donating. I think the doctor also mentioned that in the onslaught of things we talked about that day—that he was brain dead from lack of oxygen and wouldn't be the same even if he would ever wake up. It was devastating; I can't convey the utter despair and sadness we felt watching him lay there, hooked up to all those machines. Ray and Kyle kept pacing, and I sat beside him, holding his cold hand, watching for his chest to go up and down. I remember a tear or two rolling down his cheeks; it was so heartbreaking. I wish I would have had them call a priest for his last rites. It's strange all the thoughts that run through your head—I thought about his past, school years, the day he was born. I think it's a version of your life passing before your eyes, but in this case, his. I wish I would have given it a chance and put him in a room for at least a couple of weeks or longer. I wish I hadn't listened to a doctor I didn't know and called his doctor instead. I could have done that! Dr. B. told me that from what I had told him, David wouldn't have come out of it and that his heart would continue to be in arrest. Here I am making excuses for not giving him a chance to live. What life? I knew he didn't want that. He had gone through so much already.

It was the worst day of our lives! As I write this, I am crying at the thoughts of that day. I miss my boy so much that it's sometimes unbearable. Why couldn't he have passed in his sleep? It would have been terrible to wake up to find him, but at least he wouldn't have suffered. I don't imagine having your heart started six times is peaceful—far from it. I often second-guess that day. People said I did the right thing, but I'll never know! I worry he is angry with me for letting him go, but I hope not! I know he still wanted to live, do what he wanted, and go where he wanted because he had just gotten his picture taken for his passport, and a friend helped him fill out the paperwork and co-signed it for him. He wanted to go to Count Customs in Las Vegas, a car restoration place with a TV show. That would have been a dream for him. I don't know how we would have arranged that, but that was his plan. I can only hope he is there in spirit, watching all they do. Like I said, it just shows that we should not put off what we want to do because we never know when the good Lord will call us home. I wish he could have fulfilled that dream first, though. I'm sure he knew he was getting weaker and thought it was now or never. I'm so sad that it didn't come to pass for him. I'm so sorry, my love!

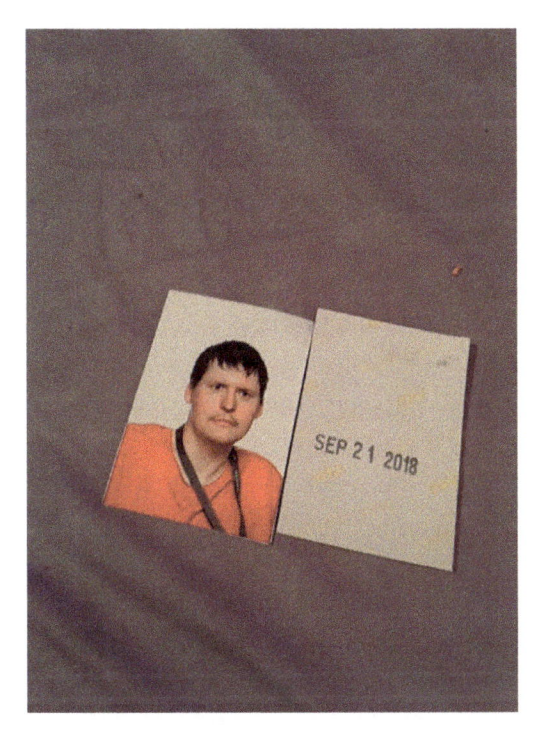

David took his passport photo just five days before his death.

Finding his passport photo after he had passed was surreal. I'm very sad that his trip didn't happen and why, but I'm glad he felt some excitement about something in his last days. Coming to terms with his absence early on was a long process; your mind doesn't comprehend that he is not in your life, in your home. You feel like you lost a limb! His life mattered so much to himself, us, especially me, his family and friends and all those whom David touched with his kindness throughout his life. The world is undoubtedly a less loving and generous place without our boy. I often use the term "is" when referring to him because if I don't, I am consciously admitting he's gone, which he is, but in everyday language, I just can't bring myself to say "was." That will probably change with time, but it's something else to hang onto right now.

Admitting that his life, the people he loved, his accomplishments, and the things in his life were over and gone is another nightmare in and of itself. That transition is still in progress. It's hard to believe that a little verb can make such a difference in how we think about something, especially something so heartbreaking. It must be awful getting to that point. There is such a finality about it, as though I'm giving up on his memory and him. If I don't say it, it isn't real. I pray for him to come home for good or at least come and see me. I tell him I won't be freaked out. I constantly ask God to bring him to me for a few minutes to show me he is at peace. Anything is possible with God! I know it's for my own selfish reasons, to make myself feel better, but it is brutal without him sometimes that I can't stand it. My God, how many times have I said that? It's so fucking hard; you just wish you could turn the clock back, but that is impossible right now. Some days are bad; others are terrible, then some more are really bad. When I'm feeling low, I like to walk to mom and dad's house, where I lived with David early on. Dad had planted an evergreen tree when David was born, and looking at it now, standing straight and tall, makes me think that's how he is in heaven right now. Memories of our time in the house are bittersweet. Knowing the tree is there gives me some peace.

When you can reach the point where you don't burst into tears the second you think of your lost loved one, you might have turned a corner on the road to finding peace. Sometimes I feel that if I don't cry for a few days, I'm doing David a disservice somehow, or that it means I forgot about him. But I know it's just healing, and that's a good thing! When you let go and cry, the tears flow hard, like wails. I had seen someone wail on a TV show, but I had never wailed before. I never understood what it meant; it almost takes your breath away. Sometimes it feels like I'm going to have a heart attack from the pain in my chest. I am reminded that the funeral home has one of those defibrillators; I wonder how many times it has been used. I can understand, especially for older people.

It's almost Christmas again, the fourth without David. It's just brutal! I thought it was hard after my dad passed in 1998; he loved Christmas so much, but being without David and worrying about Ray is too much. Ray got diagnosed with two types of cancer, both low grade, but it's scary! That and my health issues make it hard to remain positive, let alone hopeful, but what choice do I have? I just keep praying that everyone is okay, especially my Ray and Kyle. I can't lose anybody else! I hope Ray is going to be okay and he can see his mom in Newfoundland in the spring. Covid has been so tragic for so many families, unlike anything ever. Hearing about the number of cases and deaths every day is so heartbreaking. I am at the point now that I even hate the theme music the news channel came up with to pre-empt them talking about covid. I get it; it lets people know that they will be talking about the pandemic and gets their attention to listen if they choose to. I got to the point a long time ago that I couldn't listen anymore because that's all there was on the news. I'm sick of it! It brought to light the inadequacies of many of our services—long-term care, lack of nurses, and how undervalued they are. Even our grocery store workers, truckers, and delivery people were all brought to the forefront of the stage as essential workers. Late recognition for them, but it's finally there. It is such a shame that it takes tragic circumstances to recognize everyone's contributions. I would be remiss if I didn't mention the added stress for people with mental health issues, which have pushed things to a new level. These poor people had no connection to their usual outlets for help during the initial lockdowns. That must have been horrifying for them! Things are somewhat back to normal at present, but for those struggling with depression anyway, this has been just horrendous. God bless them!

I just sat down again after a few weeks to write. It's the middle of December 2021, and we are back into partial lockdown. There are lineups at the grocery stores and all the stores, for that matter. Thank goodness we got everything we needed for Christmas a while ago, so we don't have to go out for any length of time. When will all this end? It's all so devastating to everything and everyone. During this time, we've been dealing with Ray's health issues. I pushed him to get some blood work done a few months back, and it showed some trouble with his blood and the thing men hate talking about, let alone getting checked. We are waiting to speak to a surgeon and a radiologist to discuss treatment, and we are both in disbelief. It's so surreal; I'm so scared. I can't lose him after losing David, which still feels like yesterday. I must be positive for him and in our relationship, we complement each other—yin and yang. I use my strengths where he lacks and vice versa. I'm hoping and praying for the best. It gets me thinking about what would have happened to David if something had happened to Ray or myself; he wouldn't have had any choice but to be put in a nursing home. Oh my, I cringe at the thought. I wonder if he ever thought about it. He never let on, but he was always concerned about us when we were out, more than someone would usually be. He wasn't supposed to go first.

Chapter 5

I think I'm getting to the point where I'm reluctant to go downstairs. I used to go downstairs and start talking to David and do what I needed to do, but now it seems I avoid it by doing other things. Seeing his empty bed and room is a constant reminder that he is gone. Rose would say, "Get rid of it." It's easy for her and probably other people to say! I also have the Christmas lights on the balcony to plug in. I'm at the point now where I want the holidays to be over. I know that sounds terrible, but it started after my dad passed. After he passed, Kyle was born. As everyone knows, when you have kids, you tend to see things through their eyes. We tried to get into it again, but with David being gone, it seems it is something to get through. I hate saying that about the most joyous time of year, but I can't help how I feel. After this covid shit, I know I'm not alone in the loneliness of the season. It's just brutal, as though you're fighting to be happy, and the despair is kicking joy's butt! We had our traditions with David, especially with Kyle. Kyle would grab their stockings in the morning, take them down, and they would sit together, going through them and trading things if they didn't want something. David enjoyed that so much with Kyle Bear. David called Kyle a bear since he was a baby. He always wanted to spend more time with him, but because Kyle was a teenager, he wanted to do other things. He wishes now he spent more time with him like we all do when we lose someone we love. I hope Kyle knows how much David loved and adored him, like he did all his family, fuzzes included. Christmas has come and gone for another year. It's difficult sometimes to put up the tree, but I can't decide if taking it down is worse. I dread it!

One of the last photos of David's grandma and grandpa together at Peggy's Cove in Nova Scotia.

For the last few months, I've still been phoning the premier's office and emailing him to let him know what happened to David. If it wasn't for covid, I believe I'd be farther along with this or would have been done by now. I understand this is a global health crisis, but what I'm trying to do is important also. Delegate it to someone else; I'm sure there are many people on staff there. It's so frustrating. So, I soldier on. I recently found out that our local MPP must draft a piece of legislation. I already spoke to many local people; why wasn't I told this already? More passing the buck! We are in a holding pattern with Ray, thank goodness. They will monitor him for now, so back at her, I go, bugging whoever I can think of. I don't care how long it takes; I won't stop. I can't! It certainly has taken all the attention of the government officials at a time when I need them also. I get it, but it doesn't mean it's not frustrating. My God, it's been over three years since David passed. As far as covid goes, we learned some valuable lessons, like not to take our loved ones for granted and to spend more time with them, meaningful time, because you never know. Also, our planet is having a rough time sustaining our flagrant disregard for its vulnerability. We need to be more aware of our climate and try to make it a safe place for future generations because if we don't, what's the alternative? I really believe this is God's way of saying "enough." A modern-day reboot, like Noah's ark, a cleansing, as it were.

Waiting on the government is agonizing, but knowing that I got David's story out there, he was spoken about in the legislature, and his name is on the record makes me feel hopeful for the first time in a long time. I will not be ignored, and neither will the millions of people with disabilities in this country. On this particular podcast, "Troublemaker Radio," they were talking about the plight of the disabled in this country, everything from sidewalks not being accessible to doorways being wide enough. It is appalling that today, these things and others are still an issue—it's about money, of course! It's too expensive to flatten something or make something wider. It's ridiculous! David encountered obstacles so many times that I can't even count. I think that's why he was so hard on his chairs; he thought he would make the best of it and at least try to accomplish what he wanted. A lot of times, it wasn't meant to be as his chair would tip over or he would break off his footplate. He was too stubborn and frustrated. I can't imagine, nobody can until you're in their shoes, or should I say CHAIR! That's it; we should get these politicians to go around in a wheelchair for a day and try to do groceries, go into a coffee shop, or even cross a street. Let's see how they fare!

I was so anxious talking to the MPP from Ottawa since he is a disability advocate. I waited so long to have someone listen to me about what happened to David. Patience is a virtue, and I've been patient; now, I want to be relentless and troublesome. They were also talking about the Assisted Devices Program that acts as a broker between vendors and the recipients of any device they might need. They don't do much else in the way of making sure the transaction is completed and how. That would have been wonderful, especially in David's case, and maybe this wouldn't have happened. When I called them to tell them what happened with the vendor, they expressed their condolences but said they have no jurisdiction over what they do, or in our case, DON'T do. I was disgusted and enraged, to say the least. There are 2.6 million people in Ontario with disabilities and no form of oversight for what may happen to them when they get their individual devices. I hope my actions will help some other person or family not go through what we have. It's too late for David, but hopefully, it will help someone else. We also need choice. It should be against the law to have a monopoly on the industry; it begs trouble. If someone has an issue with a vendor, there is no one else to try. Tell me, is anything else like that anywhere? Every one of those people deserves better! It would be like having one doctor, one grocery store, or, to put it in David's terms, only one type of car to drive!

I had a bit of a lapse again in writing. The content is hard but necessary. I sometimes feel like I don't want to finish because I won't have anything to do. Recently, I started thinking about some other ideas for stories that David and I talked about; he had more faith in me than I do. I hope I can make him proud someday. Sometimes I even try to find odd chores to do instead of sitting down to write, which is scary! I love to see the sun, especially in the winter, but who doesn't? David loved it too. He would go out every day for a bit, but when it was sunny, he would lean back in his chair and let it shine down on his precious face. He would feed the squirrels and the birds as the sun brought them out too. He would call them and tell them he had peanuts and seeds. I still do that every day, even at the cemetery. I keep some peanuts in the truck. I still can't believe it sometimes that my boy is lying in a coffin in the ground. I know his spirit is with us, but physically, that's where he is. I feel like, who's life am I living anyway? This can't be mine. I'm in a constant state of wonder, too, like does heaven have food? Do angels need to eat? Is there music or cars? For David's sake, I hope so. Probably a lot of other people would want those things too. Are celebrities on different clouds away from normal folk? They shouldn't be; it is heaven, and we should all be equal. I wonder if David has met Bon Scott or Malcolm Young; he would love that! I like to think of my dad and David riding in some old sixties Chevy, going fishing and swimming. David was like a fish when he could swim. I remember taking him to the hotel to try and swim in the pool after he had been in his chair for about a year. He bugged me so much that I finally gave in. It was difficult because he had gained a bit of weight. I had help getting him into the pool, but it was just me in the water with him. I guess we both thought buoyancy would take over, but not so much. I lost him a couple of times under water, but I got him back up, and we used a few floatation devices, and he enjoyed it. However, he didn't ask again until we were at a beach and he was on a manual chair strapped in, and we pushed him out a bit, but he wanted to go further, so we went a little bit, and the water lifted his chair and almost turned it over. I jumped on him, and a couple of guys there helped us get him upright and back to shore. He thought it was great, but I was scared shitless! We never tried anything like that again, and he knew I wouldn't go for it again. I think he knew it was the first of a long line of things that he wouldn't be able to do anymore. You could almost see the resolve on his face, unfortunately. I tried to get him to attend the programs that help disabled people enjoy the water. I think he went once, but that was it. He wasn't much of a joiner, later he joined a group and started going downtown. They would play video games, cards, chess, and stuff like that. It was a non-profit, so they didn't have much money to do other things. It's unfortunate how many things the disabled are left out of, like amusement parks. How many rides do you think someone in a wheelchair can get on? Not many, I would imagine, not in their chairs, anyway. If someone could lift their loved one into a seat on a ride, would they have the strength to hold on? It would take someone with a lot of money and passion to create even one or two rides for a disabled person. I hope someone does someday! I heard about an inclusive park that was built in Ottawa this year—one park! Still, it's progress. David loved rides, go-carts, and anything like that. He was fearless like most kids, I suppose. Bringing them to some place where they can't participate in things is pretty much a non-starter; it just reminds them of something else they can't do. I imagine they do their best with the very little funding they get.

Since I'm no longer working, I'm not finding as many feathers and dimes as I was before. After David passed, I found them constantly. Dimes and feathers are a sign from your loved one that they are near, and you are not alone. They are supposed to bring a bit of comfort and hope of an afterlife or a message of love, hope, and peace. I think it helped me a bit, but I still sometimes wish he would visit me for a few minutes. Finding peace after losing a loved one involves believing heaven is peaceful and full of love and that our loved one is being cared for by the Father. Of course, religion plays a role in this, as I've mentioned, but depending on your religion or beliefs, I trust there is a revered being in all of them. In mine, I choose to believe David is with God and our other lost relatives, and that helps with my grief. We, the ones left behind, search for that peace as we navigate our lives without that special person or people. Losing a loved one is terribly hard, but I can't imagine losing more than one at once. I shudder just thinking about it. Getting through something like that must be heart-wrenching and never-ending. Through, not over, because

David's Heart

you never get over it. It's like a journey you're on, and you never get off the road to your destination until you meet up in heaven. Maybe that sounds corny, but that's how I like to think of it. It gives me a reason to move forward and something to look forward to. I'm always going to wonder whether I did the right thing by letting him go. He loved life, and it took him a bit to adjust to his circumstances and make the best of it, and I'm so proud of him for that! I told him that often. I'm slowly beginning to realize that after all he has been through in his life, he definitely would not have wanted to be hooked up to machines. Peace with his death and peace with my decision to let him go are things to achieve in my life going forward. They are hard but necessary goals to try to attain.

His picture from the funeral home on the speaker, of course, loaded with feathers and dimes in the morning sun.

The way things happened with the chair is the dark cloud hanging over our journey toward acceptance. Hopefully, things will change regarding that place and what they "didn't do." I will do whatever I can to change things, but I can understand those who have lost it. However, I try to find justice through writing and through phoning and emailing anyone and everyone until someone changes how the disabled are treated. David's death will mean more than just heartache and despair; it will mean positive change and justice. He would want me to keep fighting as he did. I do not want another family to go through something so tragic and senseless. Until that time comes in your life, and I hope it doesn't, you don't know how you will react. A death is terrible enough, but when it comes with circumstances that didn't have to happen, it's a whole other thing. I wouldn't wish this on anybody. We hear tragic and senseless things every day, some more lately, unfortunately, but we move on. However, when it's a loved one, it's like your pain is the only pain in the world, and you wonder why the world is not stopping. Your person is gone, so they should pay attention; why are people laughing in that crowd over there? Why are people going about their day as if nothing happened? Why aren't they upset like me? You get angry! Angry at God, angry at the world, and even angry at that person. Why did they leave me? It's all part of the grieving process, as you've heard before. The stages of grief are denial, anger, bargaining, depression, and acceptance. I think I'm between depression and acceptance. How does blame come into play? With me, it was right away. I'm on the road to acceptance, and I will end up there faster if I can get anywhere with the government.

Visiting a grave, lighting candles, and looking at pictures of your loved one are all things to help us find our peace. Grief can't be rushed; it takes how long it takes. You've probably heard people say their friends or family expect them to be okay after a certain amount of time. That is so ridiculous! No one can tell you how to feel or when to feel it. It's your grief, process, life—it's all up to you. Get help if you feel it will help you deal with your grief. Like I said before, some people don't feel comfortable discussing things with a stranger, while for others, it is best. Talk to someone—friend, spouse—when you're ready. Burdens like grief are a lot easier to carry with someone else. I must admit, the candles, visiting him, and putting things at the cemetery helped me. I feel it helps me honour him as it should. If something helps you even in the tiniest way, every day will be a little brighter. Early on, there was a darkness surrounding everything I saw or thought about. I wanted to get through what I had to do in the day to go back to being immersed in my grief. It's where you feel close to your loved one. I had a friend who lost her son to a tragic accident, and she once told me she almost looked forward to crying because it made her feel close to him. That was in response to me saying I was sick of crying. The headaches were the worst; I think it was the pressure on the sinuses. Your chest and heart literally hurt from heaving. Sometimes it's scary. I heard there is something called broken heart syndrome. Wow! It just shows you how your feelings can affect your body. It's all connected.

Days pass, months pass, then years. It's something I can't explain except to say again that sometimes it feels like yesterday, other times it feels like it's been so long. They say that God never gives you more than what you can handle! My goodness, my plate's full for a long time now, thank you very much. You look for peace wherever you can find it. Don't let anyone tell you, "Oh, that's not going to help you or change anything," because whatever you do to find peace paves the way to opening that dark curtain your brain was forced to close to help protect you at the time. Do what you need to do, say what you need to say, and it will help. Keeping memories alive is very important. It may seem hard at first to look at pictures or hear their voice on a recording, but that will change. The tears will turn into a smile the next time you go through the photo album or hear their favourite song. Good days and bad days will still be there; don't expect too much from yourself. It's a process like anything else. When my mom was taken to the hospital months ago after not being able to see her for so long, I was so worried that we would lose her that it was almost unbearable. Those who couldn't say goodbye to their loved ones in the hospital because of covid was tragic and sad. Not being able to hug and kiss her was excruciating, but you told yourself they were keeping her safe, and they did. We still don't know why she suddenly lost her ability to walk. But was it sudden? We don't know; we weren't around her. I'm sure my family isn't the only one that went through something like that, unfortunately. The nursing homes are now more open, thank goodness, and we can see her anytime, which is wonderful, but she still wonders why she is there! I told her a while ago that she must tell David how much we miss and love him when she goes. She said she would; after all, she helped raise him. He was her boy too! Thinking about the loss of another person in your life is daunting, but you know it will happen one day. At least I'll know David and her will be together.

Life's greatest mystery is death. We've all heard about out-of-body experiences. I hope the good ones are true—that it's bright and cheery and you feel elated and happy and peaceful! You see your loved ones gone before, and it's wonderful. Perhaps you stand over yourself or above and watch the people around you grieve. I like to think David is still around us here; I hope so! It helps to think that way sometimes. I still talk to him like he is still here for real. Why not? What does it hurt? Nothing. It provides comfort. Death cannot break the bond of love and commitment you have with your person.

One of my older sisters passed away almost a year ago. She was in a nursing home across town, and I hadn't seen her since covid hit because no one was allowed in. We were all devastated. I can't help but think my mother has joined all mothers who have lost a child. I know a few people who have; unfortunately, it's not as exclusive as you might think. My niece –my sister's daughter—and I have been close over the years, so I try to be there for her. It's so sad. I'll miss my sister; she was my closest sister growing up. I will remember her smile and the laughter we shared. God bless you, my dear! I can't help but feel my sister is with David and our dad. She always looked out for him and was always elated when he would visit her with us. It gives me comfort to know they are together in heaven. Her passing was the first since David, and it stirred up all those feelings of immediate sadness and despair I had deep down. There has been so much sadness the last two years, so hopefully, we are moving forward and resolving this somewhat, or at least learning to live with it. It's going to be a different world out there, for sure. With all the loss, it is hard to be grateful for what you still have, but you must be grateful. In a way, I'm grateful David was safe in heaven during all of this. I would have been crazy with fear for him during all this uncertainty. A sliver of acceptance, I guess. I was thinking the other night about how it sounds selfish when I cry and say I miss you and love you. They say we mourn for ourselves because our loved ones are in a beautiful, peaceful place with no pain or sorrow. But I definitely cry for David also; he had a lot more living to do. Things to do, places to go, people to meet, and his passport picture taken five days before his death proves that. To be taken in such a cruel and deplorable way is unfathomable. They also say forgiveness is more for yourself than the person who wronged you, but I won't be forgiving anyone anytime soon—if ever. I'll hang onto my anger; it fuels my fight for change! I hate it so much because I'm usually forgiving, but how can we forgive, especially when they have taken no responsibility? When and if they do and things change for people like David, I might entertain the idea.

Chapter 6

Gross negligence is what happened, dereliction of duty also! God, I was so stupid. I sure as hell wasn't thinking when it happened, but how can you when you're in shock? Everything happens for a reason, but for the life of me, I can't see this yet, but maybe one day I will. I'm still working with my MPP to get something like a law or an order by Health Canada to hold these vendors accountable when something goes wrong with their equipment or the people selling it. That's what they are; they are salespeople. This pandemic is still a thing, so everything is moving at a snail's pace, especially with the government. Last night, I cried for quite a while again and asked David for a sign that he was listening, and low and behold, the next morning, the first thing I saw when I woke up was a cardinal. Everyone knows it is a sign from a loved one in heaven. It gave me some peace during this tumultuous time. This is hard to write, let alone say, but I feel that losing someone you love so dearly and so close to you, like my David, renders you a little immune to that kind of pain in the future. Your heart is already broken; nothing can damage it more. David's Rose told me something similar when she gave her condolences for my sister: you feel bad and sad, of course, but not nearly as much as you did when you lost your special person. I hope that didn't sound cold, but I think it's true; you've already fallen to the depth of despair, and you can't fall any further. In some way, it may be a saving grace.

Waiting for help from the government is agonizing. I can't give up; David never did, and I can't. It's not hard to hold them accountable for their products and service like other businesses. Is that so much to ask? It doesn't make sense that they can do what they want to our most vulnerable and take advantage of taxpayers' money. It's been three and a half years; I can't believe it. Yes, I still count the days, months, and years, but for how long, I wonder? It's a coping mechanism, I guess. Wednesdays are the worst because he died on a Wednesday. I hated Wednesdays when I was a kid because my young cocker spaniel got hit by a car and died on a Wednesday. It's weird how certain things stay with you. Thinking back, I never thought about David's plot being close to mine and Ray's. It's a little far away, so I have to see if we can change the plots. People sell their plots these days; they need the money, I guess. This was just another thing we didn't think through during our anguish after his passing. You're so upset and are required to make so many decisions immediately. I can't plant anything at David's grave; there is just the vase and a flat stone. My mom had the same issue with my dad's plot; they rezoned some of the areas, and theirs were part of that. She was so upset. We didn't think to change things back then, either. I can put fresh flowers from spring to fall, which gets costly, but I always want something there. During the fall and winter, we have a beautiful orange and red poppy wreath at his grave, little things that I put there depending on the holiday, and, of course, a lantern. We had one stolen last fall; it was devastating. Who would do something like that? They are hell bound for sure! I got a new one, so hopefully, it stays put. I grew up with my mom planting things at my relatives' graves; it seems so odd not to be able to do that. You can't have anything on the stone during the summer months because they have to be able to mow the grass around the area. I've complained about black scuff marks on David's stone, and my dad's vase got broken once from them running into it with the mower, I assume. I planted two lovely bushes at my best friend's kid's big stone, and they got mowed. Just deplorable! This spring, they will be replacing them after a lot of complaining. One other time, I bought 12 beautiful orange tulips in the spring and put them in David's vase, and when we went two days later, the vase was turned over, and there was no sign of the flowers. Ray found them in the garbage, and there was nothing wrong with them. I phoned again, and they just said they would talk to maintenance. Whatever! If anything happens this year, I'm going straight to the city. That's my rant about that!

The orange poppy wreath I got for David's stone.

Rose found this growing by David's stone. It's "the star of David" type of weed— very ironic and so nice to see.

I can't stand having nothing at David's grave, but so many are unkempt. Ray said their relatives and friends have probably passed or moved away, but it's still sad to see nothing at so many graves. I believe if you are able, you should pay your respects as often as you can. I think people start that way, but life gets in the way; we are all too busy for our own good. The days go by so slowly, and we miss David so much! It's such a sense of loneliness I can't describe. Every time I look out the window, I see him booting around on his chair. It filled his days even in winter if it wasn't too cold outside. It was remarkable, but I realize now that he never verbalized how unfair it was that he couldn't walk or drive down the road, literally and figuratively. He would have had every right to complain, but he chose not to; he knew it wouldn't change anything. He had even bought hand controls for driving, a mechanism you can install in your car to use the gas and brake with your hands, thinking he would use them someday, but it wasn't meant to be, for him anyway. I ended up selling them to some young man that needed them, so at least they were used; David would have wanted that. He kept so much inside, and I think he didn't want me to be upset, or he figured what's the point in dwelling on what can't be. It was probably both. He was always my saving grace. I feel so useless sometimes, as though I have no direction, and not working anymore is just compounding the problem. I have nowhere to go, nothing to do, no one to take care of! I find myself doing too much for Kyle, which is bad. He needs to grow up and be responsible for his own life, and my hovering doesn't help. I just want to feel needed like everyone else. Taking care of David was all-consuming, but I would do it all over again in a heartbeat, but him not being here anymore is more of an adjustment than I first thought. I need something meaningful to do. I wanted to help at my friends' rescue, but they need to be able to count on someone, and with my health and general lack of sleep most nights, I'm not very dependable and don't want to put anyone in a bind.

Not having David in our lives affects so many aspects of our day-to-day lives that it's startling. The quiet is deafening, and our house and the neighbourhood are so quiet. There is nowhere to be and nowhere to rush off to; he's not here to need me. I should have taken off sooner because my body is so broken it is just unbelievable. Every time I turn around, it seems that something else is breaking down. I wonder where I'll be in ten or twenty years. Mom always says, "Look after yourself; no one else is going to," or "You can't look after your family if you don't look after yourself." She is right. I worry so much about her and her going to the other side. Even when something is inevitable, it doesn't make it easier. I miss going out for lunches, shopping, and having her come over for supper. David and Mom used to take the wheelchair taxi to Arby's for lunch occasionally; they loved spending time together.

Not that they didn't have their disagreements over the years, but not for long. I hate change; why can't some things stay the same when they are good? Unfortunately, you wouldn't know the love if you didn't have the pain. You must appreciate when things are good, but we don't do that enough. We always want something else, go somewhere else, do something else. Live in the moment and cherish the people in your life. Be present and grateful. Like a beautiful bouquet of flowers, life eventually fades, making room for more flowers to grow. I know it's a strange comparison, but all we can do is honour and love the people in our lives while we have them. Maybe that sounds maudlin, but it is what it is. I must try to do that, too, instead of wishing for the past; that doesn't get me anywhere. Wishing for David to come back is a way to keep the hope alive, and, I guess, a lifeline for me and a connection. I've asked for him to come back countless times.

My other sister, who also suffered a terrible loss, calls her stints or sessions of crying "jags." I guess it's a verb, but I don't know where she got it. I talk to her sometimes when things get to be too much, it helps to talk to someone that's been through the same type of loss, I appreciate her so much. Anyway, I just had a little "jag." I was looking at the picture of David on the fridge; he was around 10. It's a picture of him at a cemetery, ironically, and he's leaning on a gravestone. I guess they were on a history field trip or something like that at school. He was standing, but he looked a bit unsteady, so I guess it was close to when he was having trouble walking. Anyway, that's all it takes for me to cry sometimes, even after all these years. Time marches on, but the pain remains; it's embedded deep in my soul. Crying is a good thing because it releases those feelings, and you feel lighter for a while, at least until it builds up again. All I know is that remembering is good because that's all you have left. Always remember that grief is different for everyone. No one can tell you how to grieve or when to stop grieving. It's different for everyone, and so is the length of it. Never let anyone say, "Oh, you should be over that by now!" I don't think I will ever be over losing my David; it will just become a part of who I am. Since David passed away, I started to visit my friend's kids' graves again. I'm ashamed to say that it has been a while. These children, two girls and a boy, were very special to me. The youngest was born a few months before David, and we had talked about them growing up together. They were my friend's life, as our children should be. But they were taken too soon, many years ago, and to this day, I do not know how my friend got through it and continues to get through it. Something so utterly devastating happened to them that it's unfathomable. We don't talk about it much, which is understandable. What is there to say? How do you come back from that? I admire her strength and fortitude and ability to go on. It's amazing to me because I don't know if I could have. You never know what you are capable of until you are faced with it. I started taking care of the kids' stones. I planted three little bushes, one for each. I feel a little better knowing they have something there; it feels as though I'm watching over them in a way. Taking flowers and planting them where I can helps me, which is important. When I was talking about the difference in people's grief, I guess my dear friend's grief is ... what? I do not have a word! There isn't one! God bless her and keep her strong. I love you, my dear friend.

I came across an email on David's phone from a woman from OMVIC, the motor vehicle sales regulator where David passed his test to sell cars. She was wondering how he was and what he ended up doing. She was sad to hear that he had passed, of course, and told me how much she had admired his drive and how determined and invested he was in passing his test. He was so proud, and I was so proud of him. It makes me so sad all over again thinking about the future he could have had. Just when his dreams were coming true. As I was writing about OMVIC, I thought about how ironic it is that car sellers are regulated by the government but the sellers of disability aids are not. It's mind-boggling. David always waited patiently for things to happen in his life, but he had to. What choice did he have? He had told this woman about his plans for the future, opening his car lot. He was cheated on so many levels by his devastating illness. When I read what she wrote, I thought: another person touched by David. She said she thought of him often as she sees a lot of applicants, but she had never seen anyone try as hard as David or anyone who wanted it so much and was willing to work for it. He would have made a great salesman; he already was in my book, selling anything that wasn't nailed down in the garage. This led to debates like, "How much do you use that, Dad?" I can only imagine what he could have accomplished in his life, which I do very often. But imagining his future is almost torturous because we miss him so much. As I embark on my writing journey, I think about how proud he would be of his Mama Fuzz. He would have made a great teacher also; he was always so patient in teaching me things on the computer.

I spend most of my time on the internet looking for any organizations that might be able to help me. The government hasn't bothered responding yet. It's so frustrating; they work for us, right? I feel like a tennis ball being tossed back and forth, passing the buck. I guess I'm the buck in this scenario. The minister of health, deputy ministers, the premier, legislative committee members, and even the compliance board—that vendor has to answer to someone. Regulatory committees must be able to help and hopefully change things for the future of people with disabilities. During my days between writing and fighting, I go back and forth so much sometimes that I get so incensed. The people who were so ignorant about his disability and making him the butt of jokes are just uncompassionate idiots, but worst of all, not being important enough to someone to finish their job, which would have changed everything!

I don't know how or what the MPP from Ottawa has done recently to bring these issues to the forefront, but it isn't easy. There is always going to be something else that takes precedence. His office sent a letter to the vendor about David and their lack of accountability and negligent behaviour, but I guess there was no response, as I would have been told. It just shows that they don't give a shit. I hope, at the very least, it rattles them enough to look into what happened to David and watch themselves for a while until something changes. They obviously weren't following protocols or guidelines, but who works like that? I'm trying to move ahead with many aspects of my life, but this part makes me feel like we are stuck in quicksand, getting pulled out now and then but sometimes sinking deeper. I hope, for everyone's sake, we can make it out soon. Right now, I'm looking into getting information from ADP and the LHIN, which was formerly CCAC, the Community Care Access Centre. They help the elderly and the disabled find support in the community. David's occupational therapist worked out of their organization. Her job was to be David's advocate when he needed a new chair or the chest straps that tragically never got on his chair in our last dealings with her and the vendor. Over the years, she helped David with the fittings for his chair. With his height, around 6' 4", he needed a special chair, and with his double scoliosis and spine curvature, he needed special backing. I guess that is what the president of the vendor meant about David when he tried to give a faux condolence about his death but ended up vilifying him instead. He said David was a very "needy" client with all the repairs they had to do over the years and his certain specifications because of his back issues. I was so angry that if he had been in front of me, I don't know what I would have done, but it wouldn't have been good for him. Unbelievable! Had he forgotten that David was not sitting in his room, watching the world go by, but he was actually trying to do things like everyone else? David's needs were very profitable for him! How dare he! He was always full of gumption and ambition and had a strong desire to be like everyone else. His zest for life was unwavering for every day he was alive.

This book or memoir or diary, whatever it is, is evolving. It started as an homage to our dear boy and has become an account of my crusade. I wanted to get my feelings out and talk about the worst kind of grief imaginable. I wanted to tell the story of David's courage, kindness, perseverance, and the many quirky qualities he had—warts and all. The diary is appropriate for this lengthy daily ever-changing battle with grief and loss. How an individual moves forward is unique to that person. There is no set timeframe or road map in this twisting and sometimes desolate road. It is dark at times, then the clouds clear a bit, and the sun shines, which makes up for it; it's sewing a little more of that gaping hole in your heart that you've been living with for such a long time. The guilt of a laugh at something on TV or what's going on around you leaves you little by little. It was hard to imagine having a hearty laugh again back then, but it can and will happen. If that can, there is hope for other things. They say, time heals all wounds. Not true! Your wound, like mine, will not be healed, but it will become less severe, and that is a good thing; it's healing. Every day, you are not as raw as you were the day before.

This pandemic hasn't helped with a lot of things. Increased isolation has been so hard for everyone, especially people who live by themselves. I can't imagine. Just not seeing my friends for a long time was driving me nuts. We are social beings and need interaction with others; we crave it. Loneliness can play on your mind, heart, and health. Right now, things are getting better. I hope and pray it stays good, and there will no longer be more of this opening and closing of everything again. I'm grateful everyone around us has been good, but one of Ray's nephews and his son had covid, and they were bad for a while. Thankfully, they are on the mend now. This whole ordeal will leave an indentation on our lives for a long time to come or maybe forever. Godspeed to all those who lost their lives, and God bless the rest of us who are trying to move on to some sense of normal and forward. I'm so grateful that my mom made it through all this; it is just amazing! I still think about how we would have managed with David; I would not have been working, so I would have been home with him when the workers couldn't come for those first weeks when they were still figuring out how things would work with the lockdowns.

Remarkably, my mom and Ray's mom are 94 this year. Mom is almost indignant about not being 94; she thinks we are shittin' her. I actually had to do the math with her. It makes you wonder why, apart from disease and accidents, some people have such longevity. She always said, "If I knew I was going to live this long, I would have taken better care of myself." As I've said, she's been a devout Catholic all her life, so she looks forward her reward in heaven. Don't we all? She is the last of her brother and sisters, and she is the second oldest too. Maybe it's just luck. We'll never know, I guess. Knowing she won't live forever, I want to spend as much time with her as possible. I love her so much. Facing another loss is very daunting.

The fact that your loved one won't be with you anymore is a very life-altering thing to wrap your head around, which is natural. In many ways, love means pain and no more than when you lose someone. Finding things to fill my days since David's passing is something to get used to. People say, "Cut yourself some slack," or "Give yourself a break," but it's easier said than done. It's a whole different trajectory of your life; it's jarring, to say the least. You keep in mind that you are off for a reason—your disability issues—but it doesn't make it any easier, either. That is why I like to write; it helps me make sense of my feelings. I never realized or knew how busy I was before. You just do what you have to do; it's that simple. When things are done with love for someone you love so much, it's not a chore or a favour; it is just "LOVE." David used to say to me, "Can you do me a flavour?" Yes, you read that right—flavour. That was David always making a funny! I would say, "No, I won't do you a flavour, but I'll do it because I love you!" Oh my! I miss him so much! I ask myself, do I miss him more than I love him? I know it's a silly thought, but that is what I think about sometimes. I also wonder what he was thinking the day he died. Can someone think about what is happening to them in sudden deaths like that? Do they have the presence of mind? If what happened is what I think happened, he would have basically suffocated. Are your wits about you for a little bit of time, then nothing, or are you aware of everything for a long period? I worry that he was scared that he wouldn't see us again. I always wish that it was me and that he was left here without me. How would that work? I know he would be so despondent without his Mama Fuzz. What is worse: being in heaven with your loved ones gone before but without those closest to you or being left without your special person here on earth, wishing you were together? Maybe it's the same feeling of emptiness and loneliness, but in heaven, I suppose, it's better, or that's what we like to believe. Rose once said, "He is in paradise instead of being stuck here." I don't know what to think about that one. Life is what you make of it, for sure. Her feeling that way says a lot about her life and what may be lacking. I hope she finds some happiness; David would want that.

As I sit down to write, I reflect on yesterday's events. We just learned that another one of my sisters has passed away. I feel blessed that we had reconnected after many years of being somewhat estranged, which, as we found out, had more to do with other people than ourselves, unfortunately. We got back in touch a bit after David passed; in fact, she and her husband were David's Godparents. We talked for a good couple of hours on the phone and emailed every couple of days. She certainly fought hard and was so brave. I will miss her and our long conversations about "whatever." She wanted to read excerpts from this book as it were when I was just getting started. I told her she would be one of the first to read it when I was done. Obviously, that didn't happen, unfortunately. I hope she can read it over my shoulder with David and Dad. She was a staunch reader, and I wanted to show her that I had the chops for this because she never knew any of my aspirations, especially wanting to write, until we started talking again. Everything in its time. This book is important for David's legacy but not as important as trying to make changes for people with disabilities going forward, and I think she would understand that. Oh, my dear, I will miss you, and I love you! Doing what I can to fight for what needs to change on David's behalf and everything else, like Ray's health, there is not enough energy and time. It is something to lose two sisters in a year. My other sister passed two days short of a year ago. The recent losses bring all those feelings of despair back to the surface for a time, like a wound reopening. Very sad indeed. I hope they are reconnecting up there in heaven in peace. God bless you both. Take care of David for me, you two.

Chapter 7

Ultimately, it doesn't matter how or why you lost your loved one because they are still gone! You can't hug them or kiss them and share life's beautiful moments with them, but you can talk to them, tell them you love them, look at their pictures, and remember all the wonderful times you had together and maybe some of the trying times because those are the times where the love and devotion most come into play. It demonstrates the depth of love that you got through this or that. When we reflect, we are closer to that person. In many aspects of life, we learn from the trying times because it makes us appreciate the wonderful times more. Years ago, I bought one of those LED cat-shaped lights that stays white, but if you tap it, it changes colours. It's so cute, and David called it Shy 2 after our beloved real Shy. It's chubby like the real Shy! Ray eventually put Shy the cat light on one of those on and off tea lights. Later, Ray bought me a mini-Shy 2, as I call it, that I put in my mom's room. She gets a charge out of stuff like that, and I bought another full-size one for our room. I have it next to David's candle and picture, and I turn it on every night after I blow out the candles in the evening before I go to bed. I was astounded one night when I turned it on and tapped it to change colour, and it stayed orange. This happened after a bad day of missing David. It stayed that way for a while until I turned it off to go to bed. Remember, orange is David's favourite colour. Another time, it went on by itself in the middle of the night and woke me up! I know it's hard to believe, but it's true. I was told by a friend who lost her son a while before I lost David that "freaky" things would happen from time to time. One other time, his phone home page stayed on for almost an hour before I physically turned it off. As you know, the phone will go out after a minute when you're not touching it. This happened a few times. I'm not sure how, but I know why, but it's startling and peaceful at the same time. It made me think that David was with me, at least for a while. They need to let you know they are there somehow, right? I don't know for sure, but all I know is that it lifted my spirits for some time.

The cat light we call Shy2.

The dove I saw when I first woke up one morning.

One other time, I woke up, and there was a dove on my window sill. It was so wonderful to see. He or she stayed for quite a while, and I cried! Whether it was a coincidence or not, it eased some of my loneliness and pain, so I'm all for that. We strive for peace in our lives, right? Very few set out to have a life of chaos and strife. I've known a few in my life, and they are very sad. What a way to live. I've always liked to see the positive side of things, and I think David got that from me. Very rarely did he look at the negative side of things. When something bad happened, he didn't get mad. He had such a great attitude towards life. He was so special, but I'm biased, of course. Trying to reconcile the fact that someone you loved more than life itself is not here anymore is so hard from the minute you wake up to when you close your eyes and try to sleep. Sleep is almost a foreign concept, especially after losing someone. I had always had trouble sleeping, falling asleep, and staying asleep, even before David passed. Now it's just something you get used to and keep trying. I think insomnia is a normal thing when someone passes, and that is why a doctor prescribes something if the problem continues. I didn't get anything; I just stuck to my melatonin. I knew people who had issues with sleeping pills, but I didn't want anything to do with them. In some cases, if the grief is ongoing for a long time and the person is still not sleeping, they should see their doctor. I'm not a therapist, of course, but you know when someone needs extra help getting through something. There are always options out there, now more than ever. No longer are we expected to hide our feelings and lock them away; that can be and is dangerous and by no means helpful! Depression can set in so fast and creep up on you before you know it. There is no shame in asking for help with any of your feelings, plain and simple! When I was asked by my doctor and declined, she said to call her if I changed my mind. There is nothing more personal than one's grief! Even our beloved fuzzes, as David called them—Shy, our big white cat, his sister Shitara, who David called his cover girl, and Juanita, a little black and white cat David wanted from a neighbour whose cat had a litter—miss him too. Juanita was lame when she was born; I think David identified with her. She recovered quickly, but I think she still has bad memories of being ostracized by her litter mates as she is still very reserved and skittish. When David passed, she started over-licking to the point where most of her belly fuzz disappeared, and she even licked the fuzz off the underside of her paws. The vet said animals feel stress like we do. David was a constant in all our lives, so the cats must be wondering where he went. When we still had David's chair in his room, I would come downstairs and find Shitara on the back of the chair, where she would lay when he was sitting in it. It's so sad to see. Since we moved the chair to the garage, Shy and Shitara sleep on his bed. I don't have the heart to get rid of his bed. I imagine it still has his scent, so if it comforts them, it stays! I never realized that Juanita avoids staying down like she used to. Poor kitty! I sometimes wonder if animals can see spirits; I think I heard something like that. That would be great for them. I wish I did.

David's Heart

David's favourite moo Bessie and our cat Shy.

Our little girl Shitara.

David's little lady Juanita.

David holding his Juanita, named after Timothy's little Spanish cat friend in *Timothy Goes to School*.

Dealing with the sudden onset of grief is like getting struck by lightning; how it affects your body is brutal. Think about it, your heart is the most important organ in your body, and when that is "broken," so to speak, it is going to affect everything else. You are never the same—nothing is! As I said, I've had trouble sleeping most of my life, but it was strange; the first few weeks after David passed, I seemed to have slept okay. Maybe it was pure exhaustion. Afterwards, I went back to my normal restless and sleepless nights. It is fine to accept that you need help to get through something, physically or mentally, like counselling, after a death or for anything you might be struggling with. As I've mentioned, it may work for you, or it may not, but all you can do is try. Be open to it, and you just might be surprised! Historically, women are supposed to be strong and unwavering for every family member. We end up putting ourselves last in so many aspects of our lives, and that's wrong. On airplanes, they tell you to put your own oxygen mask on because you won't be able to help your kids or anyone else if you don't. We dismiss what we are told mostly out of stubbornness but we should take heed sooner, or at least keep it on the back burner.

The days are so long and the nights even longer. Not working and not having David to look after is so different; frankly, I'm going a bit nutty. Writing is tough, but I must finish. I think I'm subconsciously putting it off as a way of staying connected to David, but I need to realize that I am always connected to him. These days, my feelings are mixed up with everything else. Every feeling about every issue seems to be flowing into each other. The more I try to compartmentalize, the worse it gets. It's very strange and frustrating when you can't put your finger on the right way to help yourself. I had said to my sister once that I can't get it out of my head, that I need to be productive in some way every day. She said that I must give myself a break. Not being able to move like you once did takes a toll on what your life looked like before. It's a whole different world!

I've been watching some movies and concerts lately, which is unusual for me. David would have loved them. I remember seeing a quote a while ago about how when someone passes away, it's hard to understand how others around the grieving person can go on with their lives as if nothing had happened! When you lose someone you love, you half-expect the rest of the world to stop because yours did. It's unfathomable to see people laughing or overhearing someone talking about an upcoming wedding or birth of a baby, or vacation plans. These happy things that are the best parts of our lives leave me feeling so cheated because they aren't happening for our dear David and never will! Why him?

Selfishly or not, I also think: why us? What did I do in my past? Is this payback for something? Everyone makes mistakes in life, but as you grow, you change for the better—at least most of us do. I try not to think that God is vengeful, as it can be scary. Is that how it works? Our dear David came into this world with challenges like many others, but why does this happen? In David's case, if his life was going to be cut short because of his disorders, why did his life have to be cut short by an uncaring and incompetent person? I've mentioned that it wouldn't have been good if David's mindset was destroyed little by little. Watching that would have been agonizing, but at least he would have been here with us, and no one else would have been involved in his premature demise. One could argue that we were saved from watching him deteriorate. Does everything happen for a reason? Was he taken from us before this final destruction of his mind and soul so that we didn't have to witness this horrible and sad transformation that would have surely tainted our image and memories of him? This is so hard to write. Thinking about it makes me physically ill. Can a heart be broken repeatedly, or does each blow chip away at it over time?

What was God's plan for David and us? Was it having him show kindness to others where someone else wouldn't? That is a good legacy, and I'm so proud of him for that and many other things, but if he was a good soldier, wouldn't God want to keep him around to help others? Lots of wonderful, caring people die too soon, but why? Only God knows, but we need more of those in this world, especially these days. Alzheimer's is terrible, but dementia is a whole other animal. It's a cruel and far from peaceful end to someone's life! Why are there so many mentally destructive diseases in this world? Physical ailments are one thing, but a complete mental and personality shift where one loses the essence of who they are is the ultimate cruelty. We would have hated that to happen to David, no question. When someone passes away, many people say, "Remember them as they were." My brother-in-law said that to me about my other sister before she passed. I did not see her for a long time because of covid. He didn't want me to see her in her final days. I didn't disagree; I wanted to remember our conversations about the family, TV shows, and gossip, not how she was at the end of a long road. I guess we were lucky in many ways to have them as long as we did, but not long enough. I wonder how people feel about their life ending. I don't know how I would feel, and I pray I never do. You have your life, so to speak, but at the same time, you don't, and it's very sad. It is all about perspective! David knew he wasn't well all his life, but did it become more evident toward the end?

I think about the immense loss of life from this unbelievably unprecedented pandemic and then the daily news briefings with the shootings, stabbings, car accidents, and natural disasters. It dawned on me that every day, every minute, someone is losing someone they love. With the war in the Ukraine and other places still, it is all too much, but what can you do? You try not to think about it too much, you try not to let it impact your day-to-day life, but it's so hard when it is in your face every day. It's just an astounding concept that's been happening since the beginning of time and will continue. People will always be grieving someone— lives lived long and well, lives cut short by illness, accidents or tragedy. Everything is deeply personal to those left behind to grieve. Many believe they will see their loved ones again, and to do that, they must live their best lives. You strive for this by being a good and kind person, and that's as good as any reason to be a good person. We all say when someone is inherently mean and nasty all the time, they will "get theirs." Well, we can only hope. For them, I do not know what they are expecting, maybe a black hole of sorts, nothingness! I hope, for their sakes, it is somewhat peaceful, I guess. That's just the kind of person I am. You know when people say, "I wouldn't wish that on my worst enemy?" Well, I really mean that when I say it. I know, what a putz! I'm not meant to judge anyone; Lord knows I've made mistakes, maybe not as erroneous as others, but still. I just know what I believe, and I believe that I will see my David, my dear dad, my sisters, my dear friends that I lost too soon, and all my other relatives that have gone before. Like my mom said, "There must be something more, something to look forward to, something to strive for. If not, what is the point?"

I agree to a certain extent. Nobody is good all the time. We all have our faults, misdeeds or downright awful things that we have done to other people. Theological discussions aside, I think that is where forgiveness comes into play. If you believe in God, you seek his forgiveness, but most of all, you must forgive yourself, do better, and be better! Making amends or paying it forward is one way to change for the better. We are all flawed, and no one is perfect, but we all look for peace in our lives— most of us anyway. I wish peace for all and acceptance of loss is vital. The pain of losing a loved one, however it happened, will never totally go away. Some days it is prevalent and others not so much, but it is always relevant because your love for that person was and is. Don't be afraid to say "is" instead of "was." "Afraid" is probably the wrong word, but don't! Relevant means present, and they will always be present in your life, just in a different way. A few years back, I was trying to get to the point where I could think about David without tearing up, and I have. I wanted to think about him and smile at a memory, and I achieved that; it was a huge step forward. I thought the guilt of not breaking down in tears might be too much, but the twinges became less and less. That is healing, I guess, in some small gradual way. As I have said, staying in the depths of your grief is not healthy for your mind or heart. As hard as it seems, you must try to move forward day by day. I'm not a counsellor, but I can speak to what works for me. My mom once said, "Life is for the living." It sounds a bit strange and obvious, but think about it!

    I started a petition with change.org about bringing oversight to the vendors of wheelchairs and other disability aids, which we desperately need. Many family members and friends have signed it, together with people we don't know. I am so grateful, but it has stalled at a little over a hundred. I came across a couple of others centred around changes for something regarding disabilities and asked for advice. They told me to find some groups on Facebook to share it with. I reached out to a few, so I hope it helps to get the word out. Calling the premier's office and other government officials is getting tedious, especially when I'm being repeatedly told that it's not their problem. Can anyone ever own anything? My goodness, it's getting ridiculous, but the angrier I get, the better it fuels me to keep going! That is just what I have to do. I have no choice; it is like a mission or a calling. I can't stop. David had the stamina of a horse and the heart of an angel, so I must follow through with doing whatever I can for him and everyone else. The blatant disregard for people with disabilities is disgusting and will not stand. These people have been lied to repeatedly, ignored, and pushed aside long enough. I'm going to bring the pot to the front burner. There will always be issues that take the spotlight for a time, maybe more relevant and all-consuming, but that shouldn't mean that some are forgotten altogether.

A picture of the petition I started for change for people with disabilities. Please look it up and sign it if you are inclined.

It seems that everything I think about, even ordinary things, leads to thoughts of you, dear David. What would David say about this? Would David like how I tried to do that? David would have laughed his ass off at that! Your would-be interactions with that person are ways of keeping them in your life. I still picture David out back playing with his remote-control car, which he would do a lot to help pass the time. I love remembering now. At first, it came with pain, but now, it's a little bit of joy! I hope it never stops, but if it does, I don't know. The pain is excruciating daily, but when it eases, it is like I can breathe after being under water. I was looking for a good simile; I guess that's it. Sometimes people say that when they wake up in the morning, for the first few minutes, they perceive everything is normal, make their initial plans for the first hours of their day, and still think about their interactions with that loved one. For me, that stopped after a couple of months, unfortunately. I can't tell you how sad that was. These days, especially in the spring, I look at the sky and say, "Good morning, my David, the orange in the light in the sunrise." I miss his beautiful smile in the mornings. He never woke up grumpy. I hate not seeing his face anymore or hearing his voice and laughter. The grief is only outweighed by the anger I feel. I know I am not alone in that. I can't imagine what the grieving person of a loved one lost to violence must feel every day. It can be a cruel and unjust world for a lot of us. Time goes too slow for many and too fast for others, usually depending on the situation, but time is something you can never get back or have enough of. Time is also a saving grace. When you lose someone, it marches on and slowly chips away at the dark cloud surrounding you until one day, you start to feel lighter, and your outlook on the rest of your life doesn't seem so foreboding. It does and will happen, but you must let it because that is where you find some guidance. It will get better, and I believe that wholeheartedly. Always remember that your loved one loved you too. Tell yourself that they wouldn't want you to be in this darkness for the rest of your life. No loved one would.

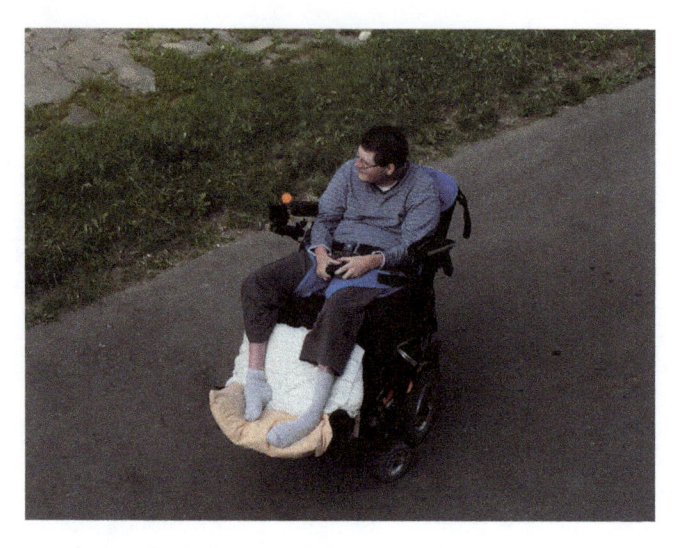

David playing with his remote control car.

I picked "David's Heart" as the title for my first book to reference his enlarged heart from the Friedrich's and the huge heart he had in his all too short life. His humanity and compassion for others made his heart huge in every sense of the word. David was (I still hate saying that word) a kind, silly, giving, and compassionate soul. He was caring and empathetic, almost to the point where it was detrimental to him. He had a warm and inviting personality that, if given the chance, he would have been your best friend, and you'd be a lucky person indeed! David wasn't given that chance very often, but he overlooked that and moved on. I think that was one of his greatest qualities; he was very patient. I think he had to be given his circumstances, but as I mentioned before, many others might have gone in the opposite direction and been angry and bitter, but not our boy! I know the praise of a mother for her son, but I know more than anyone else that David wasn't perfect; nobody is. However, in my book, and it is in my book, he came damn close. I could go on, but it is still difficult to think about all his wonderful qualities without getting choked up, missing him as I do day after day. Your feelings can dictate how you go about doing anything in your day. How can they not? They are a part of you, and you make decisions based on them or not. They affect how you look at things that happen to you or others. It is strange and sometimes foreboding, but it can't be helped; they are a part of you and will shape your conscious and unconscious thoughts. I hope I explained that correctly as I am having a hard time with the ending of this homage to our dear David. I told my friend that many people think that the beginning of a book is hard to write, but it isn't; it's the ending! How do you sum up what you've been trying to convey to people about your topic, in my case, our dear son, his life, his struggles, his demons but most importantly, his HEART? I hope I did him justice and told his story with a fraction of the love he had for his family, friends, and fellow man.

Again, it doesn't matter how or why you lost your loved one; they are still gone! You can't hug them, kiss them, hear their laugh, and most of all, share a life with them. What you can do is still talk to them, and I wholeheartedly encourage you to do so. I talk to David all the time about our TV programs, articles in the paper, cars, and what's going on in our lives and the world. Tell them how much you love and miss them. They will hear you; I firmly believe that! Look at their picture often and recall the wonderful times you had together, especially the laughter, and you will be surprised as a smile starts to form on your face. It is so helpful, believe me! If you recall a trying time in your life with your loved one, embrace that also; we can learn from that. After all, that was part of their life, and somehow you are brought closer to them still. It will and does make that person not seem so far away.

Going forward with my quest for justice for David, with the hope that this doesn't happen to any other family, I will continue to advocate to make the appropriate parties be held accountable as they should have been all along. It would be wonderful if someday there was a "David's law," a mandate or law that protects people with disabilities. Just like the nursing homes need an impartial person to oversee the day to day of what goes on, someone from the March of Dimes or Easter Seals or some organization like that needs to oversee the transactions with the vendors and their clients. I shudder to think about what goes on with them and a client that can't speak for themselves and has no one to speak up for them—someone that isn't out for the almighty dollar, as, unfortunately, most companies are. The ADP needs to be abolished or restructured. People need to know that ADP has no say in how the vendors treat you. They have minimal protocols or standards; I wonder if they have a mandate at all! People go to them for help, and no one cares or listens. Well, they are going to listen to me!

THERE IS NOTHING MORE PERSONAL THAN ONE'S GRIEF. MINE IS SPECIAL AND SPECIFIC TO ME. YOURS IS YOURS AND YOURS ALONE. TAKE ALL THE TIME YOU NEED TO BE OKAY. IF YOU ARE BETTER THAN OKAY, GREAT, BUT DON'T RUSH IT! AT THE END OF THE DAY, FIND PEACE WHEREVER YOU CAN AND ALWAYS KNOW THAT IT'S OKAY NOT TO BE OKAY, BUT NOT FOR TOO LONG. ABOVE ALL ELSE, DON'T CLOSE OFF YOUR HEART; OUR DEAR DAVID NEVER DID! BE WELL AND LOVE ALWAYS; THAT'S WHAT OUR HEARTS ARE FOR, AFTER ALL!

THE END (FOR NOW)

"We will miss you and love you forever and a day, our dear boy."

"You are my love and my light; I miss you with all my might."

"The morning light through the window that lights up your smiling face on a candle only lasts a little while, like the time you were here with us."

"You were my sunshine, my lovely sunshine, you made me happy when skies were grey. You'll never know, dear, how much I love you, why did you have to go away?"

Completely orange tree near David's stone at the cemetery the fall he passed.

Memoriam picture from the newspaper for David.

The Christmas cross we got for his stone for the holidays.

David's Heart

My dresser with all his pictures. It all helps!

The story link picture about David that was in our newspaper a few months after he passed.

Laurie O'Brien

The spring after David passed, my orange impatiens overflowed.

David and his little girl Juanita. He loved her so much.

More Images of David:

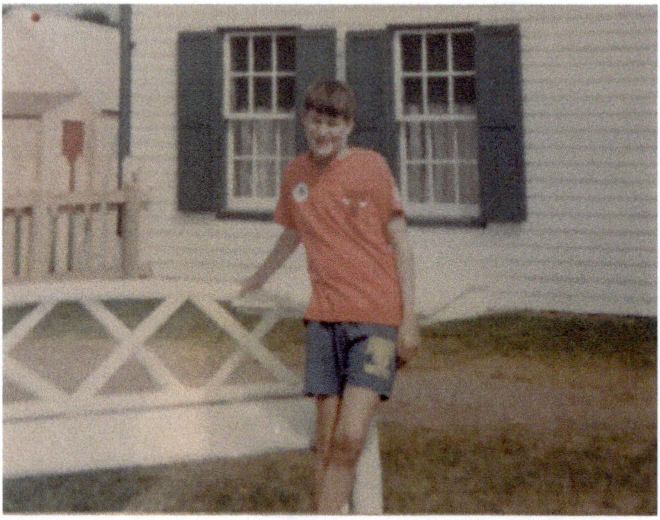

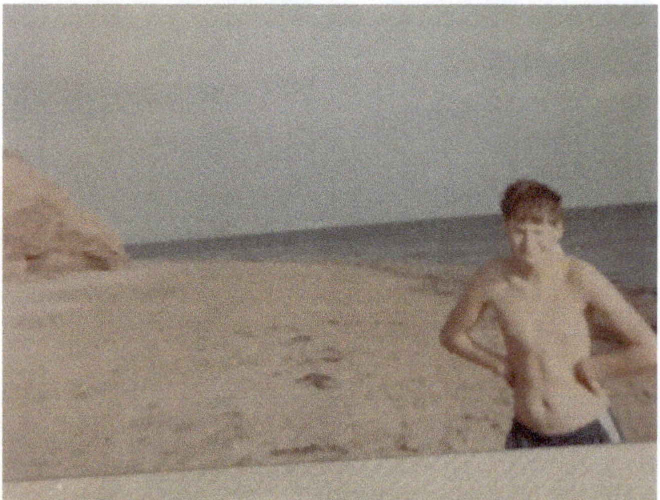

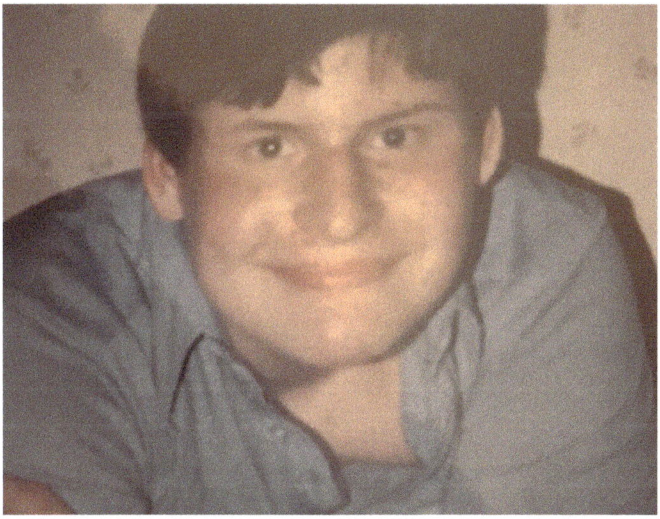

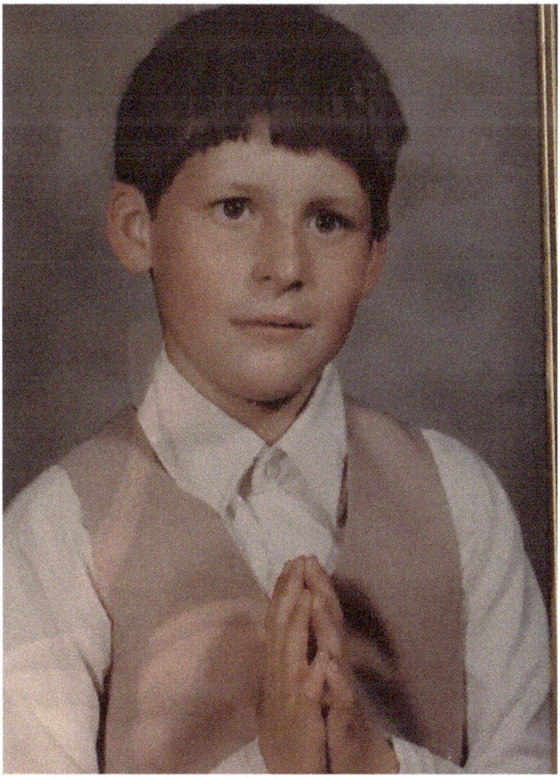

CPSIA information can be obtained
at www.ICGtesting.com
Printed in the USA
BVHW092138301022
650606BV00005B/18

9 780228 881209